Miracles

Do

Happen

Hope you enjoy it

EConnors

Eileen Connors

Table of Contents

Acknowledgment

To my beloved family, cherished friends, and the supportive community at the Elks Lodge, your unwavering presence and encouragement have been the guiding lights that propelled me forward.

I owe an immense debt of gratitude to the esteemed medical professionals who played pivotal roles in my healing journey. Dr. Kelly and Dr. Earl Farnsworth, DC, NC, Dr. Fleming, NC, and Dr. J.R. Stober, DC, NC, your expertise, dedication, and compassion have not only saved my life but have also granted me the opportunity to thrive. Dr. Kelly, Dr . Earl Farnsworth, and Dr. Stober were Naturopaths and Chiropractors, and Dr Robert Fleming was a Naturopath.

I count myself incredibly fortunate to have been surrounded by such an exceptional group of individuals who stood steadfastly by my side through every triumph and tribulation. Your unwavering support has been the cornerstone of my resilience and the source of my greatest strength.

Chapter 1

Trigonocephaly

I came into this world as Eileen, the second daughter of Ben and Diane Peterson. The year was 1958, and it was a Monday in April when I made my debut at the Old St. Mary's Hospital in New Westminster, British Columbia, Canada. My roots were a tapestry of Norwegian, Scandinavian, English, and Irish heritage, weaving together a rich ancestry. My mother stayed at home and raised the family, my dad was a logger and worked in and out of town.

My sister Kathy was 15 months old by the time I joined the ranks. My early days were marked by a stark departure from the norm. Almost immediately after my birth, both the doctors and my parents were confronted with my physical deformities, which set me apart in a unique way. I faced challenges that were truly exceptional, as I was unable to move my arms or legs, my head was like a misshapen egg, my eyes were misaligned, my cheekbones, the bridge in my nose, and the roof in my mouth the bones had not formed yet so were not visible, because of this I could not through my nose.

The diagnosis was clear: **Trigonocephaly** (tri-gono-ceph-aly), a condition with a name as intricate as its effects, means a "triangle-like" shaped skull. It's characterized by a ridge protruding from the forehead, often resulting in closely set eyes and a pointed, narrow forehead.

This rare developmental defect during embryogenesis was a result of the premature fusion of the metopic suture, a term derived from the Greek word for "forehead." This fusion led to the distinctive triangular shape of my forehead with an obvious or subtle osseous ridge. It also brought with it transverse growth restriction and parallel growth expansion, which resulted in developmental delays.

The cause of trigonocephaly is not yet known, but possibilities could include genetics, the type of medication the mother takes while pregnant, and the position of the baby in the womb.

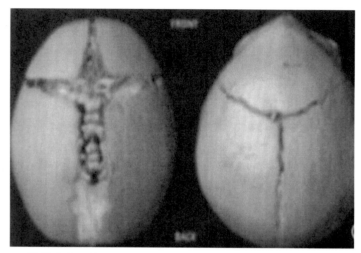

Skulls before birth open skull is normal, closed skull with point is mine

5 months old quadriplegic

Chapter 2

Finding Treatment

In my case, I am the only known instance where Trigonocephaly was combined with quadriplegia, further adding to the rarity and complexity of my condition.

My journey was set on a path that was anything but ordinary, marked by medical intricacies that would shape my life in ways I could never have anticipated.

My early life was marked by a profound sense of uncertainty, as my physical challenges remained a puzzle with no clear solution in sight.

My parents and the medical professionals who cared for me were understandably concerned and uncertain about how to proceed. They began to explore potential remedies. As they grappled with my condition, the doctors embarked on a search for other cases like mine. They discovered babies with similar head deformities, but no one with quadriplegia, but the proposed surgical solution was fraught with risks. It involved cutting the top of the skull and inserting different sizes of metal plates as the skull grew to allow for reshaping of the head and promoting brain growth while minimizing potential brain damage. However, the surgery held no guarantees, and the odds of survival were uncertain.

Faced with this daunting decision, my family ultimately chose not to proceed with the surgery as the risks outweighed the potential benefits. It was a difficult and courageous decision, given the life expectancy for a child in my condition was less than two years without the surgery. I was merely four weeks old, and the prospect of being placed in Woodland (Hospital) in New Westminster, BC, which was a facility for children with a developmental disorder, was looming just two weeks away.

My family was determined to explore every avenue, leaving no stone unturned in the pursuit of a solution in their commitment to finding an alternative path that would offer me a good quality of life. The pursuit of a brighter future only began with countless unknowns.

Time was of the essence, and my family's desperation for a solution was palpable. My grandmother, a pillar of strength, turned to faith and the network of people around her to find a lifeline. She prayed fervently and enlisted the help of others in our quest to unlock a path forward. With each passing day, the urgency grew.

In her determined search, my grandmother reached out to her chiropractor for guidance. It was a fortuitous conversation, as he mentioned Dr. Farnsworth, a name that would ultimately become a beacon of hope in our journey.

The chiropractor made contact with Dr. Farnsworth, who was residing in Kamloops, B.C., and sharing the intricacies of my situation, and to our relief, Dr. Farnsworth occasionally visited his friend Dr. Robert Fleming in Surrey, B.C., and agreed to meet with us at Dr. Fleming's office during his upcoming visit to Surrey.

He was also a glimmer of opportunity. The prospect of this meeting was like a lifeline thrown into the sea of uncertainty.

The days leading up to our appointment with Dr. Farnsworth were filled with a sense of urgency, as we knew that time was not on our side. My grandmother and my mother were eager for the day to arrive as the weight of our circumstances bore down on all of us.

The day finally came when we met with Dr. Farnsworth and Dr. Fleming. They set their eyes on me; they were struck by what they saw. Their collective years of practice and expertise had never brought them face-to-face with a case quite like mine. At that moment, a sense of hope and possibilities began to permeate our journey as we embarked on a path guided by their unique perspectives and dedication to finding a solution.

Dr. Earl Farnsworth, spurred by the unique challenges of my case, reached out to his fellow friend, Dr. Richard Stober, who resided in Portland, Oregon. As he shared the details of my condition, Dr. Stober's amazement mirrored that of Dr. Earl upon first seeing me. In response to my situation, Dr. Stober recommended a technique that he had developed and specialized in from the 1940s until his passing in 1987 – the Bi-lateral Nasal Specific Cranial Technique.

This technique is a controlled approach used by Chiropractors that works to unwind the body and help it return to a more optimum function by adjusting the cranial plates of the skull and relieving pinned-up pressure that affects the nervous system and reestablishes the flow of cerebrospinal fluid to the body and the proper flow of blood to the brain.

This technique aims to release the sphenoid bone and allow the cranial sutures to move freely, permitting the brain to circulate fluid and nutrients from the top down. The hope was that this would alleviate pressure on the brain and spinal nerves, allowing for a more unobstructed flow of energy.

This technique, often simply referred to as "the Cranial," had initially been designed to treat infants and children facing a range of head trauma-related challenges from birth, such as cerebral palsy, autism, ADHD, hearing loss, and more. It was a non-invasive procedure that involved the use of a blood pressure ball, a finger cot (a small surgical balloon), and a toothpick, along with a piece of thread to wrap around the finger cot once it's placed on the blood pressure ball, ensuring it wouldn't release during the procedure.

For my family, this technique came as a beacon of hope. With the decision not to pursue surgery, Dr. Stober's Cranial technique emerged as a potential answer to our prayers. The prospect of being placed in Woodland (Hospital) was looming, and time was running out. It seemed that a miracle had been sent in the form of this innovative and non-invasive procedure.

As the treatments were to begin immediately, a new challenge emerged. My mother was confronted with the daunting task of covering the expenses associated with our frequent travels between Vancouver and Kamloops via train, as well as accommodation and other added costs. The financial burden was substantial, and the stress it brought was an additional overwhelming burden.

In our hour of need, we turned to the Elks Lodge, a fraternal organization dedicated to supporting and promoting community needs. Their mission revolved around providing charitable assistance for families and children facing challenges, just like ours. It was a pivotal moment when the Elks Lodge stepped in to help us, providing the much-needed financial support that would enable us to focus on the treatments and wait for the transformative changes in my condition.

The weight of financial concerns had lifted, allowing my parents to breathe easier and fully invest their hopes in the progress that was unfolding.

Chapter 3

Treatments

At the tender age of six weeks, I embarked on my first treatment at Dr. Fleming's office under the expert guidance of Dr. Earl Farnsworth. Dr. Robert Fleming observed Dr. Earl's work closely, actively learning the technique, which allowed him to continue the treatment when Dr. Earl returned to Kamloops.

The procedure was an intricate one involving a finger cot (a small surgical balloon) that was securely tied to a blood pressure ball. The purpose was to carefully navigate one finger cot into one of my nasal passages using a toothpick and then apply controlled pressure by inflating the finger cot to approximately 40 pounds of pressure. The goal was to assess the condition of the nasal passages – there are six in total, three on each side (upper, middle, and bottom).

Dr. Earl would systematically release the valve on the blood pressure ball, gently withdraw the finger cot, and move on to the next nasal passage. The procedure was repeated until all six passages had been evaluated. What he discovered was disheartening: my nasal passages were locked, unyielding, and resistant to opening. This procedure, which demanded great precision and patience, took a minimum of one hour to complete, if not longer.

In a testament to Dr. Earl's commitment to exploring all possibilities of opening up the passages, he would try twice in each passage, then go to the next passage until he completed all six passages, and when I returned the next day, he would try again.

The intensity of the treatments prescribed by Dr. Earl demanded a great deal from my tiny body. After each session, he recommended that I get a full night's rest, ideally between eight to ten hours. The treatments were extensive, and the resulting adjustments left me profoundly fatigued. It was a matter of allowing my body to relax and allowing the effects of the treatments to settle.

The treatment plan was structured around one session per day, conducted three times a week for a total of two weeks while Dr. Earl was in Surrey. In the initial week, Dr. Earl employed a gradual approach, starting with a single finger cot in each nasal passage. Over time, he increased the number of finger cots by stacking them atop one another. This method was designed to exert a controlled and progressive force on the passages he was working on, with the goal of opening them.

In the early days, a few of the passages remained obstinate and did not open, which presented a concerning challenge. However, the unimaginable occurred during the second week. Dr. Earl continued to increase the number of finger cots, eventually reaching three stacked on top of each other. The culmination of this effort was that most of the passages were fully opened. It was a remarkable transformation. After these two weeks of intensive treatment, I experienced a profound shift in my condition. I could breathe through my nose and slowly nurse from a bottle, and the roof of my mouth and the bridge of my nose slowly began to develop as nature had intended.

The strength and pressure that Dr. Earl applied to open my locked passages truly defied belief. It was nothing short of miraculous, a testament to his unwavering dedication and, one could even say, divine intervention.

The commitment to my treatments was unwavering, but it posed logistical challenges for my family. Since my mother didn't know how to drive, my grandmother stepped in as the dedicated chauffeur, driving my mom and me from Burnaby to Surrey for the treatments. The journey took an hour or more each way, disrupting my grandmother's entire work schedule. As a result, she was only able to make this trip three days a week.

Dr. Fleming, who took on the role of administering my treatments in Surrey, adjusted the approach out of concern for my well-being. He inserted only three finger cots into each of my passages instead of the need to increase the number of finger cots that Dr. Earl would do. After three months of treatments, Dr. Fleming advised us that he was no longer able to proceed with treatments. This was due to his compassion and his reluctance to watch me in my pain and discomfort. This left us with no other option but to travel to Kamloops for two weeks each month, where Dr. Earl continued the treatments. During these two-week sessions, I received treatments twice a day, five days a week.

Chapter 4

The Journey to Kamloops

Our journey to Kamloops, a city where we sought the expertise of Dr. Earl, began with a trip to the Vancouver Train Station on Hastings Street in Vancouver, B.C. The train ride to Kamloops was a substantial nine hours long, and after a few trips, some of the conductors recognized our unique situation and kindly encouraged us to go up to the dome car. This provided a quieter and more comfortable environment, allowing my mother and me to find some much-needed rest and sleep during the journey. It was a thoughtful gesture that made our travels more manageable, providing us with moments of privacy and tranquility amidst the challenges we faced. My grandmother would stay at our home during the day until my dad got home and look after my sister while we were in Kamloops.

Dr. Earl's office was a modest space conveniently located across from the train station in Kamloops; it offered easy access to all the amenities we needed during our visits. Our lodging at the Princess Hotel, which was situated next door, made our stays in the city all the more convenient.

Each visit to Dr. Earl's office was accompanied by a familiar and challenging routine. As soon as I heard Dr. Earl's voice, I couldn't help but start crying. The memory of the previous treatments lingered in my young mind, and the fear would set in. My mother played a crucial role in comforting and calming me down during these sessions, providing the support I needed to get through the treatments. The dedication and care of both Dr. Earl and my mother were instrumental in guiding me through this arduous journey, even when the process was challenging and unsettling.

Dr. Earl's approach to my treatments was a carefully calculated one. Each visit, he would begin with two finger cots and gradually increase the number at each session to assess how many were needed to keep the nasal passages open. If, at the next visit, the passages closed up, he would revert to the number that had worked in the previous session and then slowly add one finger cot at a time until the passages were open. It was not uncommon for the passages to fluctuate, considering that this was all new territory for my developing skull, and my treatment sessions were now limited to two weeks instead of the previous months' worth of treatments.

As the months passed, the dedicated care and adjustments made by both Dr. Earl in Kamloops and Dr. Fleming in Surrey began to yield results. By this time, Dr. Earl was using five-finger cots. The placement of my facial features started to slowly shift and become more stable, and I found myself able to nurse from a bottle better.

5 months old quadriplegic

1-year-old

1-year-old

1 ½ years old

5-year-old

5 years old. Pointed forehead, uneven eyes

Dr. Earl's patience and kindness shone through as he worked with me, attempting to alleviate my discomfort and tears during the treatments. With time, the progress was evident. My cheekbones, the roof of my mouth, and my eyes started to take shape and maintain their positions. The prominent peak on my head began its slow descent. My mother's determination was unwavering; she knew the road ahead would be long and challenging, but she was ready to do whatever it took to help me.

A remarkable turning point occurred when I was approximately five months of age. Dr. Earl's persistence paid off, and he was able to continue increasing the number of finger cots until he reached an astounding total of 12, one on top of the other, which he inserted into each passage. This marked a significant breakthrough, and after a few weeks of treatments, I began to regain the ability to move my arms and legs. With this newfound mobility, I could now soothe myself by sucking my thumb and kicking my feet. The excitement about my progress was palpable, and anticipation filled the air as we wondered about what would come next. There were moments when the passages would close and other times when they would remain open, but the overall trajectory was undeniably positive.

As Dr. Earl's treatment continued, he maintained the use of 12 finger cots until he felt that the passages would remain open and allow the skull to slowly settle into its proper alignment. This would take about two months of treatment. With the skull becoming more stabilized, he gradually reduced the number of finger cots, eventually reaching a point where four or five were used in each nasal passage.

Though late, this allowed me now to try crawling, which was a slow process that took about three months as I had to learn about balance coordination and finally figure out how to move my arms and legs for the first time to move anywhere. It also took longer to learn how to walk for the same reasons. Mom said that I was also very unsure of myself, and she was happy that I was trying and could not wait til she did not have to carry me anymore. And she could look forward to the day that we could walk together.

I can just imagine all the stress that my mom was enduring watching me go through all these treatments and thinking of how I felt during the procedures. But it finally paid off and the end result now was a true glimmer of hope that the future would be good. Mom was able to relax, and now we could both spend our time together and put the stress behind us.

The uniqueness of my situation became apparent as we delved into the intricacies of my skull. It was likened to a jigsaw puzzle, where the bones should interlock with one another, providing stability and structure. However, in my case, the edges of the puzzle were smooth, lacking the usual interlocking mechanism that held them in place. The bones were present, but without the typical interlocking edges, there was nothing to keep them in their proper alignment.

Remarkably, I can recall moments from my early months, even when I was about six months old, during the course of my treatment. It's worth noting that babies as young as six months can form both short-term and long-term memories. While my short-term memory might be less reliable, my long-term memory has proven to be remarkably acute. This recollection is a testament to the lasting impact of those early experiences and the incredible journey that has shaped my life.

As I grew older and able to understand instructions, Dr. Earl introduced an added level of caution to the treatments, which involved my active participation. He asked if I could hold my breath during the procedure. This precautionary measure was essential because if the finger cot(s) were to inadvertently release from the blood pressure ball and enter my lungs, it could have fatal consequences.

The treatments I underwent were certainly not pleasant, as when the finger cot was pumped, it would expand and go through my nasal passage and down into my throat, which made me feel like I was choking. This discomfort was the reason I had to hold my breath during the procedure. However, it was a necessary means to confirm that the nasal passages were open, which, in the long run, was good news. Initially, it was a challenging experience, but with time, I adapted and grew accustomed to it.

When I was about one year old, I was so proud to walk into Dr. Earl's office. Seeing me walking, he showed surprise and happiness.

To make the treatments a bit more manageable and offer some comfort, Dr. Earl would reward my bravery and cooperation with a vitamin C candy as a treat after each session. Following the treatment, my mother and I would return to the hotel so that I could get some rest. Upon waking, my mother would take me to the store across the street, where I had the delightful privilege of choosing one or two items as a reward for my good behavior. The options usually included a puzzle, a game, or a coloring book.

These items served not only as rewards but also as tools for learning and bonding. My mother and I would engage in activities together, with her coloring alongside me and participating in games and puzzles to facilitate my learning process. Jacks, in particular, held a special place in my heart. This game demanded coordination and concentration as you placed small metal star-shaped objects (jacks) on the table, bounced the ball, and aimed to pick up as many jacks as possible before the ball bounced again. The incremental challenge of picking up more jacks with each attempt made it a fun and engaging exercise in skill and dexterity. These moments were not just about entertainment but also a way for my mother and me to connect and support my development in a nurturing and loving environment.

Dr. Earl's insight into my future added another layer of amazement to the journey. He confidently predicted that I would grow to be tall, slim, and wear glasses. The sheer accuracy of this forecast was astounding, leaving everyone around me in awe.

The treatments continued for two weeks a month until I started school. Then, the schedule would change to one week a month, two treatments a day for five days. At this point I asked Dr. Earl Farnsworth if I could call him Dr. Earl as it was easier for me, and he agreed, and we both chuckled.

Chapter 5

Starting Elementary School

During my early years, our family resided in a cozy three-bedroom house nestled in the heart of Coquitlam, British Columbia. It was a practical and welcoming home, complete with a dependable wood-burning furnace in the basement that kept us warm during those chilly Canadian winters. The house had ample space for our growing family and a vast, fenced backyard where we spent countless hours at play, exploring the world as children do. Life was marked by simplicity and the beauty of everyday routines.

My early years were marked by a certain level of clumsiness, primarily because my coordination was still developing. In one instance, I was walking up the front steps at home and fell and split my head open. That resulted in my Parent's taking me to the hospital for stitches. Upon arriving home, I did the same thing, but this time, there was not enough time since last fall, so I could not get stitched up again. Other visits to the hospital included such mishaps as after falling out of a wagon and breaking my collarbone, I would come home, fall again, and break the other collar bone. The frequency of my accidents raised suspicions among the doctors at the hospital, who began to wonder if I was being subjected to abuse. Concerns were expressed, with the doctors cautioning that my frequent head injuries could potentially lead to cancer or brain damage.

In response to these concerns, my grandmother took action and crafted a helmet out of Styrofoam, which I had to wear for a year. This protective measure was deemed necessary until my coordination gradually improved. Fortunately, by the time I started kindergarten, I was no longer required to wear a helmet. These challenging and formative experiences were a part of my early journey, shaping the path to the remarkable progress that lay ahead.

The commencement of kindergarten was a significant milestone for me and my family, marked by the arrival of my baby brother, Carl. By this time, all my facial features had formed and remained in their proper places, with the exception of the pointed forehead. I appeared perfectly normal, sporting short hair with bangs that gracefully covered the pointed area. The teachers at my school were aware of the challenges I faced, and they made commendable efforts to accommodate me during this transitional period.

The prolonged presence of the pointed forehead had a significant impact on my development. It had caused pressure on the brain, hindering its growth and ultimately slowing down the learning process. Understanding the importance of addressing these concerns when I was five years old, my parents took me to a pediatrician, Dr. Robert Dunn, in Vancouver. Over the course of a couple of years, Dr. Dunn guided me through various tasks, including matching shapes, colors, pictures, and counting.

Dr. Dunn's assessment and findings were then sent to our family doctor, Dr. Joan Ford, who practiced in New Westminster, B.C.

Dr. Robert Dunn's approach to my condition left many questions unanswered. He couldn't fathom why there seemed to be gradual improvements in my condition without any significant changes to his methods. My family chose not to disclose the alternative care I was receiving from Dr. Earl because Dr. Dunn held a different perspective. His disbelief in naturopathic approaches meant that the true source of improvement remained hidden from him.

As Dr. Dunn observed the subtle but consistent changes in my condition, he inquired with my mother, asking if we were seeking care from other doctors. He was curious about the changes he noticed, and this curiosity led to probing questions. My mother, however, didn't see the need to divulge the full extent of my treatment. She asked, "Why?" when questioned about seeking care elsewhere. Dr. Dunn's response was rather disheartening. He shared his prognosis, stating that based on his findings, he believed I would face significant intellectual challenges, might not complete school, and would ultimately lead a life as a "nobody."

As I grew older, I became increasingly apprehensive about continuing to see Dr. Dunn and expressed my discomfort to my mother. We decided to discontinue our visits to him, a choice that brought me immense relief.

At 7 years old with cheeks, after treatment

Once again, we continued to board the train in Vancouver and head back to Kamloops for another round of treatments. It was always interesting to see how my skull progressed during the time between visits. The treatments were now spaced to every four months, consisting of two sessions per day, five times a week, and spanning one week per month. During these treatments, I had to hold my breath while Dr. Earl applied pressure to the blood pressure ball, causing the finger cot to expand, signaling the successful opening of the passage. However, not all passages were consistently open, and Dr. Earl would patiently adjust his approach to address this challenge.

On occasion, while inserting the finger cots with the guidance of a toothpick and applying the necessary pressure, the toothpick would accidentally puncture the finger cot, leading to the need to start the process anew. The energy and effort required by Dr. Earl to consistently apply pressure across all six passages was evident, as his flushed face and exhaustion revealed the demanding nature of the procedure. I once asked him if I was too much for him, and we shared a lighthearted chuckle. Dr. Earl's kindness and patience were enduring qualities that made the journey more bearable and hopeful.

Dr. Earl noted that my skull was stable but required a bit of tweaking, which was positive news.

Kindergarten marked the beginning of my formal education, and it was a half-day program held every morning. Conveniently, we lived within walking distance of the school, so my mother and I would join other parents and children as we made the pleasant walk to and from school each day.

I vividly remember the routines of kindergarten, where we sat at our desks and used high books to create barriers around our work areas, preventing distractions and interactions with others. Our morning was taken up by counting, coloring, and familiarizing ourselves with the alphabet, including a snack break and outdoor playtime. Afterward, we would come inside for a nap or quiet time on mats with blankets for another half-hour and finish the day by listening to the teacher read to us.

One of the highlights of my day was the outdoor playtime, during which we often played tag. This activity helped me immensely, enhancing my coordination, strengthening my muscular structure, improving my concentration, and allowing for socialization with my peers. I would find that I would tire quickly after running, so I told my mom about it. She asked me if it happened daily, and since it did, she took me to the Doctor, and they realized I had a heart murmur and was not allowed to participate in any strenuous activities.

Grade one brought a new set of challenges, but with the support of my teachers and my mother, I managed to navigate through it.

Grade two posed new challenges, I found it difficult but struggled through it. It was during this time that I was enrolled in tap dancing lessons and five-pin bowling, both of which were intended to assist me in improving my memory and coordination ability. While I continued with bowling, which became an enjoyable activity, I pursued it into my 30s, and tap dancing eventually lost its appeal. The intricate steps and memorization required for tap dancing became too confusing and challenging for me!

A notable concern during this period was the discovery of a bone protruding on the inside of each of my feet. My mother, attentive as ever, took me to see our doctor, who could provide a referral to an orthopedic surgeon. The appointment was made, and the time finally came to see the surgeon, who was very informative, as he observed the protruding bones on the inside of my feet, along with flat feet (lacking arches) and bent toes in which I was walking on the top of the toes. His assessment was sobering; he informed my mother that I would require surgery in a couple of years because I was deemed too young at that moment. He also recommended the creation of customized shoes to accommodate the protruding bones.

My parents took me to get my customized shoes, which now would allow room for the bone to grow if it needed to, and they felt more comfortable walking in and without any pain.

It was time to go back to Kamloops again. My father, who had some time off, drove us to Chase, B.C., where Dr. Earl had relocated to his house, about four miles outside of Kamloops.

The visit proved to be quite remarkable. My skull had remained stable, and Dr. Earl advised my mother that I wouldn't need to return unless any issues arose, suggesting that we could consider checking back in six months. This news brought me a sense of contentment and relief.

I helped my dad build a fire pit in the backyard. My job was to bring him the red bricks from the back fence and leave the others behind. This experience filled me with happiness, as I felt valued and useful.

However, an incident occurred when my brother, who was about two years old at the time, observed our dad throwing wood into the fire. In an attempt to imitate him, Carl gathered whatever he could find and began tossing it into the fire. We soon realized that, in his enthusiasm, he had inadvertently thrown one of my specially-made shoes into the fire. Oh, No!!! He was not allowed to help anymore.

Animals were a cherished part of our family, and my parents instilled in us a love and responsibility for taking care of them. We had some rabbits and a black lab named Pal, and our parents taught us how to properly care for these furry members of our family.

My dad took it upon himself to teach me how to look after the rabbits. We were especially excited when we learned that our rabbits were pregnant, anxiously anticipating the arrival of the bunnies. Before the bunnies were born, we had to separate the male rabbits into another cage to ensure they wouldn't harm the newborns. Once the bunnies arrived, we covered their cage to keep them warm. These tiny creatures were about three inches long, with no fur, delicate pink noses, and tiny furless feet that could feel sensations. I took my responsibility of caring for them seriously, and my mother taught us how to handle the feeding and cleaning of the pens. This experience provided a valuable opportunity to witness and share in the wonder of new life with animals.

My friends were just as eager and excited as I was to interact with the rabbits and their babies. However, we had to limit visitations of the number of friends at a time to two at a time, as the presence of too many visitors could make the mother rabbit nervous, potentially causing her to harm her babies.

When I reached grade three, our family relocated to Burnaby. In our new home, we had a three-bedroom house that was heated by a wood-burning stove in the basement. My dad would order wood and have it delivered. My older sister and I were responsible for helping bring the wood into the basement, where it could be piled and used to keep our home warm during the colder days. This shared responsibility taught us the value of working together and contributing to our family's well-being.

Our new property was quite spacious, featuring numerous fruit trees and room for a garden. This allowed us to embark on a journey of learning how to cultivate various vegetables and fruits, including peas, carrots, corn, beans, and potatoes. In addition, we had apple, plum, and pear trees that added to the variety of our garden. It was fascinating to witness the entire growth process, from planting the seeds to seeing the crops ripen. And, of course, there were times when we couldn't resist sneaking out to enjoy some of the fresh vegetables and fruits straight from the garden. I remember indulging in a few fresh carrots as I picked them and helped my mother gather vegetables for our dinners and fruits for our lunches and snacks.

One of the most enjoyable aspects of gardening, especially for me, was the process of harvesting potatoes. I loved pulling the potato plants out of the ground, with help, and then digging deep and wide to find the potatoes hidden beneath. It was crucial to make sure I gathered every last one of them to prevent new plant start-ups as winter was coming. What I found particularly intriguing was that potatoes didn't just stay close to the plants like other vegetables; they had the ability to travel some distance underground. This treasure hunt for potatoes involved making tunnels in the soil to locate them. This activity was not only a lot of fun but also provided an opportunity to get dirty, play in the dirt, and further develop coordination, memory, and concentration.

It has been six months since the last treatments, so now it's time to go and see Dr Earl again. He applied three finger cots and gradually got to four finger cots, and all the passages were open. This was the happiest day for us all. Now, the skull and body had accepted the new placement of the bones. It was now up to me when I felt I needed treatment. Mom was especially happy as the train ride was getting to her, and now we can stay home for a while.

Walking to school became a daily routine, and we often stopped to pick up friends along the way. Our path took us alongside a large ditch, where the water tended to remain stagnant and had a distinct smell. This ditch was a favorite spot for muskrats, which added a unique element to our journey to school.

Our daily walk to school wasn't always without its challenges. One of the older children who accompanied us, Bobby, had a tendency to be a bit of a bully and tease us about wanting to push us into the ditch. Fortunately, his threats never materialized into actual actions. Bobby had a penchant for mischief, often pulling pranks on people and even the teachers. Some of his stunts included placing frogs in the teacher's desk drawer or wearing a snake wrapped around his neck to school. We made it clear that we didn't appreciate his pranks, and he eventually stopped. Surprisingly, over time, we managed to put those differences behind us and became good friends.

In the midst of all this, my mother discovered that I needed glasses, which was an adjustment in itself. Later, we found out that the shifting and realigning of my eyes due to the treatments had caused stigmatism.

Transitioning to a new school brought with it a series of adjustments: new teachers, a new environment, new classmates, and now, glasses to get used to. It was recommended that I do extra homework to help me with memory and comprehension and continue my daily routine around homework—I'd start with it in the morning, have breakfast, go to school, return home to continue working on homework, have dinner, and finish off with more homework before bedtime. Elementary school was a bit of a struggle for me, and in grade three, I had to enter a special class for slow learners, which consisted of about five other children. This arrangement provided one-on-one teaching to help us catch up at our own pace. Fortunately, I only needed to stay in that class for one year before returning to regular classes.

From grade four to grade seven, I was able to remain in regular classes. During this time, I didn't have many friends because I was primarily focusing on my schooling and continued to ask for extra homework. My sole aim was to prove to both the doctors and teachers that, through hard work and determination, I was capable of achieving anything.

Mom and I continued to go to Kamloops on a yearly visit just to maintain the stability of the skull until grade seven. Thankfully, all the passages were staying open and everyone was very happy.

I remember sharing with my mother that when I grew up, I aspired to become a Naturopath. I wanted to help others just as they had helped me. This goal remained my unwavering focus.

The rest of elementary school continued to present its challenges, but my determination and persistence never wavered. With this determination and will to succeed, I was able to progress through each grade, always aiming for that ultimate objective.

Chapter 6

Foot Surgery

At the age of nine, a visit to the foot specialist marked a significant turning point. During the examination, the specialist matter-of-factly stated, "Now we will do surgery." It was then revealed that the tendons in my toes were misaligned, prompting a necessary intervention. The procedure involved a meticulous approach - each protruding bone was shaved off by half an inch. The realignment of these bones and the strategic repositioning of tendons over the shaved surfaces aimed to rectify the anatomical anomaly.

The surgical correction wasn't just a matter of physical adjustment; it held the practical objective of creating arches in my feet. These arches, once properly established, played a crucial role in straightening my toes. Interestingly, there was a subtle mention that this misalignment played a part in the development of my birth defect.

During the initial phase of recovery, my education took on a different form. A dedicated teacher came to our house to ensure that learning didn't take a backseat during my healing process. My wheelchair had a board that started on the seat that I sat on and extended out inorder to keep my legs straight out infront of me. My feet remained in a straight position for a prolonged eight weeks. The simple act of putting my feet down was strictly off-limits, making daily activities a carefully orchestrated routine of sponge baths and being tenderly carried into bed.

Navigating the confines of my home presented an unexpected challenge. Walls and people became unintended obstacles as I clumsily wheeled through the house. Remarkably, my frequent collisions never incurred reprimand, adding a touch of humor to an otherwise trying time. The wait for the casts to come off felt interminable, but the prospect of freedom brought with it a new set of challenges - learning to walk again.

The transition from casts to unrestricted movement meant starting from scratch. Whether it was crutches, a walker, holding onto my mom's reassuring hand, or finally venturing to walk independently, each step in the journey required patience and persistence. After eight weeks, a significant milestone was reached – a return to school. The personalized, one-on-one teaching I received during this period became a crucial catalyst, propelling me to catch up with my classmates swiftly.

Despite the progress, a persistent memory problem lingered, presenting an additional hurdle.

I had to have my feet molded for arch supports. This was a messy task that looked like I was putting my feet in cement, but it was not. I waited a week for them to set and then went back to get them fitted for my feet. I first realized that they were painful as it felt like I was walking on a hard ball. I knew this would help my feet develop properly, so I gradually got used to them. I had to wear these for about one year, and they graduated into a pair of fiberglass inner soles, which were made similar to the cement but with fiberglass, and I wore them for eight years.

Chapter 7

Gaining More Responsibility

As I navigated the challenges of daily life, my older sister assumed the role of a vigilant guardian, ensuring my safety in the face of increasing chore complexity. One vivid memory involves our reliance on an electric wringer washing machine, a mobile apparatus with a basin and agitator designed for efficient clothes cleaning. The two rollers perched above the basin served the crucial function of wringing out the freshly laundered clothes.

Our laundry routine was a meticulous process: clothes, soap, and water in the basin, setting the timer, and, once done, feeding the clothes through the wringer and swiftly retrieving them on the other side. Occasionally, a stubborn piece of clothing would necessitate the lifting of a lever on the side of the wringer, popping it open to free the trapped fabric and resume the process. After washing, the cycle continued with draining the soapy water, refilling the basin with fresh rinse water, reintroducing the clothes, agitating to rid them of soap, and setting the timer once more.

The culmination of this effort saw us meticulously placing the freshly washed clothes into a basket, ready for my mom to carry them upstairs to the back porch, where they would hang on the outside clothesline.

Once the laundry had dried, my mom would efficiently retrieve it from the line and usher it inside. In a routine that unfolded with methodical precision, she'd summon me, saying, "I'll show you how to fold the towels and where they go, and that'll be your task come laundry time."

Engaging in this responsibility proved to be more than a household chore. Folding towels became a regular exercise that not only contributed to retaining muscle strength but also fostered a sense of accomplishment, increasing my memory storage and allowing me to remember more than one thing at a time and concentrate. The rhythmic repetition of this task embedded a practical routine in my daily life.

For a considerable stretch, everything proceeded smoothly, each laundry session seamlessly blending into the next. However, life, in its unpredictability, threw an unforeseen challenge our way. It was a day like any other until my sister, Kathy, inadvertently found herself entangled in the electric wringer. Panic ensued as her urgent cries for help pierced the air, "HELP, HELP!" Drawing my mom downstairs, the gravity of the situation unfolded before us.

When the unexpected unfolded, and my sister inadvertently thrust her arm through the wringer, my mother's composed voice cut through the panic. "Try to stay calm and still," she instructed. With a swift motion, Mom pulled the lever, lifting the rollers and freeing the arm. A stroke of luck spared her from any broken bones, although regrettably, this incident wasn't a singular occurrence. Lessons were learned, and her resolute declaration, "I learned my lesson, always pay attention," echoed with a newfound awareness.

In the backdrop of these moments, I would often find myself uttering, "Mom, I forgot how to fold the towels." Her patient response became a familiar reassurance: "I will show you again, and then you can do it." This exchange marked the beginning of my involvement in household chores—a source of satisfaction and a platform for learning.

As the art of folding towels became second nature, my repertoire expanded. Gradually, I found myself folding not just towels but an array of items, though sheets remained a formidable challenge for a while.

Chapter 8

The Unexpected

A seemingly innocuous invitation from our friend Sherry next door to pick cherries unraveled into an unexpected twist. Eagerly accepting, Kathy and I joined her, blissfully unaware that what we thought was a cherry tree turned out to be a poison ivy tree. The revelation of our mistake elicited a collective "Oh No!" from us all.

The hospital became a familiar destination once again, this time for a different reason – to undergo stomach pumping after ingesting poisonous berries. Doctors swiftly inserted tubes down our noses to our stomachs, efficiently extracting the harmful contents. That ill-fated encounter with the toxic berries ensured we never ventured near that tree again. An experience etched in caution.

Amidst the ebb and flow of family life, a moment of joyous anticipation unfolded in our living room. Mom gathered us kids and, with a glow of excitement, revealed the forthcoming addition to our family by showcasing her growing belly. The guessing game ensued: would it be a boy or a girl?

The countdown to the new arrival was marked by occasional requests to feel the baby on Mom's stomach. Then, the joy reached its peak when I felt a little kick. Ecstasy fueled our curiosity, prompting each sibling to seek the elusive sensation. The magic intensified when we all succeeded in feeling those tiny movements. This newfound connection with the impending arrival led to a routine of gentle teasing – a collective insistence on feeling Mom's belly whenever the opportunity presented itself. As the delivery date approached, our eagerness manifested in another request: we would lay on her belly and feel movement, a gesture of excitement amplified by the fact that I was now ten years old and could understand what was happening.

The anticipated day arrived, introducing us to our newest family member, a little baby sister named Barbra was born. She was distinguished by her vibrant red hair—unique among us siblings because the rest of us were blonde. Despite my suggestion to name her Rosemary in homage to her distinctive hair color, Mom and Dad remained steadfast in their choice.

As Barbra grew a bit older, Kathy and I eagerly assumed the responsibility of looking after her, assuring Mom that she need not worry about a thing. That idyllic sentiment, however, met a swift reality check with the arrival of dirty diapers. The swift retreat from our initial commitment was marked by a candid acknowledgment: this wasn't a task we were cut out for.

With the expansion of our family, Carl maintained his own room. Upon Barbra's arrival, she nestled in Mom and Dad's room until she reached the age where she could comfortably sleep on her own. Eventually, she transitioned to sharing bunk beds with Carl, favoring the bottom bunk for her slumbers. The ebb and flow of family dynamics continued each chapter, unfolding with its own set of practicalities and shared spaces.

In our shared room, Kathy and I each had our own single beds. One ordinary day, the impulse to take an afternoon nap led me to inquire with Carl about the possibility of occupying the top bunk. His casual agreement paved the way for a seemingly routine break.

However, that nap took an unexpected turn. Abruptly waking up on the floor, I found myself screaming, prompting a swift response from Mom and Dad. The cause of the commotion became evident – I had fallen off the top bunk, my middle finger bearing the brunt of the impact. The injury traced a path from the top left of the middle finger on my right hand, cutting across the fingernail and descending down the right side to my finger. Puzzled, Mom and Dad searched for blood all over the bunk, but the source of the injury remained elusive.

A quick trip to the hospital ensued, with Dad taking the wheel to get me the necessary stitches. The incident left an indelible mark, not just physically but psychologically. The fear that gripped me in that moment prevented any future ventures to the top bunk. To this day, the mystery of what caused the injury on that seemingly innocuous bunk bed remains unsolved.

Dad, an avid fishing enthusiast, extended an invitation to Carl and me to join him on a fishing trip with our neighbor, Bill. With the promise of an adventure by the Fraser River, we eagerly accepted. Little did we know, it was sturgeon fishing that awaited us. Undeterred, we embraced the challenge of digging our own worms, baiting our own hooks, and managing our catches with a little help from Dad. That day, fate handed me a remarkable experience - a tug on Dad's line, escalating into a struggle that compelled me to pass my rod to Bill for help. The unexpected revelation of a 12-foot sturgeon at the other end left us all astounded. Getting it into the boat and then having to put it in the truck and get it home became a feat in itself, and the communal effort from neighbors was required to hoist the massive catch into the house. Dad, with a surgeon's precision, carved the colossal sturgeon into steaks, but the culinary excitement was short-lived as its taste proved less than palatable. The unanimous decision echoed: no more sturgeon fishing for us, a pledge to pursue trout or salmon instead.

Under the Pattullo Bridge in New Westminster, BC, Dad continued our fishing expeditions. The sandy surroundings allowed us to play while anticipating the elusive bite. Starting with kids' fishing rods, we gradually graduated to adult ones. However, the plea to use Dad's rod for a chance at a big catch was met with a paternal refusal - "It's too big for you," he would insist. We enjoyed this fishing trip and found it to be the best place to catch fish.

As tradition dictated, when each of us turned 12, we were granted the opportunity to choose a musical instrument. While my older sister opted for the accordion, my own desire for the same was redirected by Mom. I settled for the guitar, embarking on a year of lessons. However, the intricacies of memorizing notes and chords proved to be more than I could enjoy, leading me to abandon the musical pursuit.

Chapter 9

Facing Obstacles in Quesnel

Dad's job opportunity in Quesnel prompted a significant change for our family. Leaving behind the hustle of Burnaby, life in Quesnel offered a more unhurried pace and a more budget-friendly living environment. Our first home in this new town was a sevenplex, where seven units were attached together. It served as our residence for a couple of years until we found a suitable piece of land on which to build our own house.

Grade 8 pointed forehead

Upon our move to Quesnel, Dr. Earl Farnsworth from Kamloops recommended a Naturopath who happened to be a friend of his and conveniently lived just two blocks away from us. I explored a couple of treatments with the Naturopath but didn't find the confidence I was seeking. Turning to Dr. Earl, I sought his guidance and continued when I needed my treatments with him in Kamloops.

When I started high school, the frequency of treatments was adjusted to assess the stability of my skull. Recognizing the signs for treatment became second nature for my mother and me; agitation and loss of temper signaled the necessity, accompanied by subtle shifts in the positioning of my eyes and the concaving of my cheekbones. The protruded peak in my forehead, thankfully concealed by my hair, remained a constant. The relief for my mother came not just from the progress in my condition but also from the reduced travel, allowing for a more settled and progressive phase in our journey.

Embarking on grade eight brought a new routine: catching the bus at the end of the road. The journey was filled with excitement, providing an opportunity to converse with friends and others until the designated stop arrived.

Junior High School, which spanned from grade 8 to grade 10, posed a distinct challenge. Mom, ensuring transparency, communicated about my birth defect and the accompanying challenges. However, despite the elementary school's commendable report, the label of "dumb" from the teachers persisted. Undeterred, I recognized the academic path as crucial for my aspiration to become a Naturopath. Despite their doubts, I persisted, facing hurdles as my course selections were frequently altered with discouraging remarks like, "You're too dumb for those courses."

Transitioning from elementary to Junior High School proved arduous due to the elevated difficulty of the courses. Fully aware of the challenge ahead, I resolved to give my best. A brief stint with French revealed the difficulty of memory work, leading me to opt for practical courses like cooking, sewing, typing, and shorthand, in which I excelled in the courses. Biology presented an insurmountable hurdle with its extensive memorization, resulting in failure. English, too, posed difficulties with the intricate rules, making book reports a daunting task. Despite these struggles, I somehow managed to pass.

My Junior High School routine mirrored the discipline of my elementary homework schedule. Days were dedicated to studying, homework, and chores, leaving little room for social events or friendships. Every year, when course selections loomed, the recurring comment echoed, "You're too dumb for academic courses," so I remained on the basic course selection, and with unwavering persistence and diligent effort, I passed each year.

I found that, with the stress of school, it was time to go back to see Dr Earl. Mom and I packed our clothes and got ready to go to Vancouver Train station again and board the train to Kamloops. This time, I was older, which made for a pleasant trip, and I was amazed at the scenery. I believe it has been at least a year since the last treatment. I explained the problems that I was having with my stress level, harder workload, and memory problems. He then started with three finger cots and found out, YES, that some of the passages were blocked. Mom and I stayed in Kamloops, having two treatments a day, five days a week, for two weeks. He would increase the finger cots as needed to six, and then the passages became stable.

At the age of 15, during my ninth-grade year, our family found a promising six-acre property on the other side of Quesnel. The dense treeline enveloped most of the land, leaving a central acre, including the driveway, for our envisioned home. As funds became available, Dad initiated the gradual process of teaching the family how to build the house.

My involvement began to help my older sister and dad with nailing plywood to the floor joists. The task demanded precision, as I had to navigate the gaps between joists to avoid the three-foot crawl space below and ensure I didn't miss the nail and hit my fingers. Beyond the construction skills, this work provided benefits in concentration, memory, coordination, and arm strength.

Once the floor was securely in place, Dad, my older sister, and I moved to ground level to construct the rafters.

Dad, ever watchful, asked me about the number of nails I hammered in the rafters, to which I humorously responded, "I do not want the roof to fall down." The work was not just a responsibility but an enjoyable and engaging experience.

Subsequently, Dad enlisted our help in constructing and installing frames for the room dividers in the house. As the rafters were completed, Dad and I returned to the floor, coordinating with the rest of the family to lift the rafters from the ground to the floor. The collective effort aimed at making the house ready for occupancy before the onset of winter became a shared endeavor that brought us closer together.

Dad enlisted a friend's help to erect the rafters on the room dividers and install plywood and shingles on the roof. Windows and doors soon found their places, with sheets serving as temporary dividers between bedrooms and the bathroom.

Learning the ropes of building a house proved valuable, enhancing my coordination, concentration, and physical strength. However, the cows in the vicinity had different plans. They regularly tore pieces of tar paper, unraveling the house's exterior until we eventually were able to put siding on the house.

Moving day arrived, though the house was far from completion. The kitchen boasted a wood stove, while the living room had a wood heater. The absence of running water, a toilet, or a bathtub lent the feel of camping to our new abode.

It had been six months since we last saw Dr Earl, so we were hoping everything would be good during this visit. He started with three finger cots and found that there were more open passages, so he slowly increased to six, and things were stable, but we still needed to come back every six months.

Grade 10 commenced in our partially finished house, marking a shift to Senior Secondary School and signaling an end to the constant changes in schools. Despite encountering a mindset reminiscent of Junior High School, I remained undeterred and focused on my goal. In grade 11, the math teacher allowed me to take trigonometry on a trial basis, surprising everyone—including myself. Despite missing algebra and geometry prerequisites, I persevered and passed, an achievement that marked my graduation. While my grades settled at a C average, the satisfaction of passing overshadowed any concerns, reinforcing my pride in my accomplishment.

Fetching water became a regular ritual for Kathy and me. Dad would drive us to the creek half a mile away, where Kathy navigated a small hill to gather water in buckets. Passing them up to me halfway up the slope, I then handed them to Dad, who was by the truck; he would empty the water buckets into a 30-gallon container. This routine continued until the container was full. The journey home was followed by the transfer of water from the truck to another container in the house.

Winter brought added challenges as the icy hill to the creek became treacherous. We endured numerous falls while lugging the water, repeatedly questioning Dad about when we could have running water at home.

Bathing was a unique adventure. Water for baths was heated on the woodstove in the kitchen and then transported to the vast tub in the bathroom. The process was time-consuming, and by the time it was my turn, the water had often cooled considerably.

The completion of the house marked the beginning of a series of additional projects on our property. Dad felled trees and cut them into firewood. We diligently stacked the wood in the woodshed and filled the wood box in the house, ensuring a steady supply of the woodstoves.

With the house now standing, our attention turned to constructing a barn and a chicken coop. The homestead expanded to include chickens, pigs, cows, turkeys, and two horses.

Dad took the time to teach me the art of milking cows, a task that proved challenging initially. It took a while before I got the hang of it, but once I did, the best part of milking revealed itself – engaging in playful milk fights with both my siblings and the cows. The cows, in their own way, communicated their impatience with our antics by kicking the pail, dipping their hooves into the bucket, or swishing their tails in our faces. It was as if they were saying, "Stop playing around and get the job done."

The responsibilities of caring for the animals fell upon my siblings and me. Milking the cows, collecting eggs, and ensuring the well-being of the various animals became integral parts of our daily routine.

The culmination of the milking process involved bringing the milk bucket to the house, where it cooled down before undergoing the next stage. Mom skillfully skimmed the cream from the top of the milk and placed it in a jar. The creation of butter was a collective effort – two individuals seated at opposite ends of the table rolled the jar back and forth in order to make butter. The end result was a reward in the form of fresh milk, cream, and butter. Beyond the sustenance it provided, this task became an excellent opportunity for me to enhance my coordination and concentration.

While my siblings quickly caught on to the chores, I required more supervision. Mom, with her firm but nurturing approach, declared, "After school, everyone is going to help with outside chores." Despite the workload, I found solace in the routine. Morning tasks included feeding and watering the animals before school, while the more demanding chores awaited us upon returning home. Cleaning all the pens, providing food and water, and, in the winter, carrying animals into the house became part of our post-school routine. Fortunately, not all the animals required attention simultaneously, offering a bit of relief in managing the responsibilities.

Winter brought new additions to our homestead in the form of baby chicks, turkeys, and piglets. The cold weather made it impractical to keep them in the barn, so they came into the house. Our household operated on self-sufficiency, deriving sustenance from everything we grew and, unbeknownst to us, almost everything we raised.

The sight of these tiny creatures running around the house delighted us, prompting the hopeful question to Dad, "Can they stay in the house always to stay warm?" Dad's response, a blend of practicality and humor, informed us that as they grew bigger and messier, the barn was the more suitable abode. Once they gained a bit more strength, the chicks, turkeys, and piglets were relocated back to the barn.

The extent to which the pigs would grow was a surprise awaiting us, a realization that unfolded as they progressed from adorable piglets to considerably larger animals.

The completion of the barn was a milestone, providing shelter for all the animals in all weather conditions. Collecting eggs from the chickens became one of my assigned chores, and it was an adventure navigating the various places where the eggs could be found—outside in the pen, in nests, or sometimes just on the floor. The occasional discovery of double yolks, two eggs in one, added an extra layer of excitement to this routine.

When the pigs were pregnant and nearing the time to give birth, Dad issued a stern warning to stay away from their pens. Weighing around 400 to 600 pounds, the protective sows posed a potential danger. However, under Dad's supervision, Kathy and I were allowed into the pen to bring food for the sows. This practice taught us responsibility and allowed us the privilege of observing and sometimes allowing us to hold the newborn piglets.

Being present during the butchering of animals was another part of farm life. Barb's innocent idea of using a chicken intestine as a skipping rope added a touch of humor to the serious task. The decapitated turkeys, in their final moments, would create a lively scene, attempting to land on our backs as we ran from their flapping wings.

Following the processing phase, our duty involved immersing the turkeys and chickens in hot water for a brief period, followed by carefully extracting them from the heated water and removing their feathers. This was a very smelly process. The objective was to prepare them for dinner, a task that I found less appealing when it meant consuming the same creatures I had cared for.

Questioning Mom about the type of meat on the dinner table revealed a necessary but uncomfortable truth—we were eating animals we had raised, even some that were once our pets. Initially reluctant, we eventually grew accustomed to the reality of farm life.

Flicka, my horse, was around three years old, and I was the only one in the family who could ride her since I was lighter. Riding her taught me valuable lessons in control, patience, responsibility, and calmness.

Despite the enjoyment I found in riding Flicka, others in the family weren't as fortunate. When Dad or the rest of the family attempted to ride her, they would inevitably be bucked off. While I secretly reveled in having a horse all to myself, we did have another horse that everyone could ride, except for Mom, who preferred observing our equestrian adventures.

Flicka and I had a unique bond. Riding her bareback with just a halter, we would trot and gallop down the street, enjoying the freedom together. Flicka had a dislike for walking, a preference that suited me just fine. Our rides were filled with joy and laughter, and she particularly enjoyed being brushed and having her feet cleaned, activities I gladly spent time on.

Sadly, Flicka's temperament changed over time. She became aggressive towards others, especially the farrier, making it necessary for me to part ways with her. It was a difficult decision, as I cherished the bond we shared. Despite the challenges, the short time I spent with Flicka left a lasting impact. She helped me develop balance, concentration, muscle strength, and coordination, for which I would always be grateful.

Later, I learned that Flicka had been abused as a colt, which explained some of her behaviors. The day we tried to load her into the trailer was emotional, with Flicka kicking at the door in fear. It was a sad day for all of us, particularly for me, as I said goodbye to a horse I loved deeply.

The task of fetching water from the creek became such a laborious chore that Dad decided to simplify our lives by having a well drilled. When asked how he located water, the well driller interestingly explained that he used a divining rod or "witched" for it. He demonstrated by holding a "Y"-shaped branch, advising that branches from witch hazel or fruit trees worked best while advising against using willow branches as they did not work. As he walked the property, the stick flipped upside down in his hands, signaling the presence of water below. The next day, drilling commenced, and we had a well, eliminating the need to trek to the creek for water.

With water now piped to the house, we enjoyed the convenience of running hot and cold water. The luxury of individual baths replaced the communal trips to the creek, making daily routines more comfortable.

In the winter, our neighbor, a trapper, crafted snowshoes for each of us from beaver hide. While I found snowshoeing enjoyable, the exertion was surprisingly strenuous, revealing a new perspective on physical activity.

Living in Quesnel provided a unique learning experience that would stay with us for a lifetime. The slower pace and distinct way of life shaped our understanding of resilience and adaptability.

Chapter 10

After Graduation

Upon graduation, I proudly presented my diploma to my doctors, specialists, and high school teachers, showcasing my achievements. Among my accomplishments was trigonometry, a subject I tackled without prior algebra or geometry. The surprise and amazement from those who doubted my ability in academic courses served as a testament to the power of perseverance and determination. Their apologies and genuine happiness for my success highlighted the importance of defying expectations and believing in one's capabilities

Grade 12 graduation

May 16, 1977

Miss Eileen Peterson,
R.R.#3, Rawling Road,
Quesnel, B.C.

Dear Eileen:

Thank you for your letter and the good news that you graduated from High School last year. I remember you very well, and I am just delighted that you have done so well. It just shows that the old saying is true: "where there's a will, there's a way". The condition you had was trigonocephaly, myopic astigmatism (are you wearing glasses?), poor posture with somewhat lax muscles, and mild foot deformity. There were also some learning problems, and I think you are to be congratulated on having overcome all these problems so successfully.

Dr. Don Forbes has been unwell and is not yet back at work, but I shall be glad to let him have your good news by sending him a copy of this letter.

I hope we may meet again sometime, perhaps when you have become an x-ray technician.

With best wishes,

Sincerely yours,

H. G. Dunn, M.B., F.R.C.P.(Lond. & C.),
Professor, Department of Paediatrics.

HGD:GRW
c.c. Dr. D. E. Forbes

Dr Dunn's apology letter after graduation.

76

Despite facing challenges in high school, particularly not passing biology, I remained unwavering in my pursuit of becoming a Naturopath.

Dr. Earl's early prediction about my physical development proved accurate—I graduated standing tall at six feet but with a weight of only 90 pounds, giving me a distinctively slender frame coupled with glasses.

While traveling to Portland for university exploration and to gather information about schooling, I learned about Dr. Richard Stober, a Naturopath in Portland, Oregon. I seized the opportunity to make an appointment with Dr. Stober for a cranial treatment. His surprise at seeing me was evident, as he had heard much about me from Dr. Earl Farnsworth. Receiving treatment from Dr. Stober was a source of pride, marking a unique moment in my health journey. While I never returned to him, I was confident in having one of the best doctors in Canada—Dr. Earl Farnsworth, who, when retired, referred me to his son, Dr. Kelly Farnsworth, also a Naturopath practicing in West Vancouver, BC.

My initial foray into the working world commenced with a part-time position in Quesnel. The job involved on-the-job training to become a legal stenographer at a lawyer's office. I transcribed dictation, converting spoken words into written form, covering documents like wills, mortgages, and liens. The process involved using a Dictaphone, similar to a cassette tape recorder, where lawyers recorded their instructions. I would then listen to the tapes with headphones and type out the dictated content. Despite completing the training, my employment was intended to remain part-time.

In a strategic move to enhance my skills and increase my employability, I opted to attend a vocational school in Burnaby, B.C. The goal was to further refine my business and office expertise, eventually securing full-time employment in my chosen field.

I packed my bags and moved to my grandparent's home in Burnaby, B.C. Eager to enhance my business skills, I decided to enroll at Vancouver Vocational School and completed a one-year secretarial course in Burnaby, BC.

My grandmother was so proud of how far I had improved and of my accomplishments. She wanted me to have a good start in life. It was my wise grandmother who nudged me towards a new opportunity – a job at the British Columbia Telephone Company (BC Tel). Surprisingly, I landed a job in just three days because of my typing and shorthand skills. With a knack for typing at a swift 60 words per minute and shorthand at a blazing 100 words per minute, I was all set.

But here's the twist – I never found myself in the stereotypical secretarial role. Computers became my domain, and I delved into tasks far from the typewriter and shorthand pad. BC Tel had this policy where you could shuffle around different roles and still hold on to your seniority.

My journey within the company was like a rollercoaster. I dabbled in Advertising, crafting bill inserts for telephone bills that showcased our offerings. In Engineering, I tackled plant maps and sketched out subdivisions, deciding where those vital telephone cables should snake through the land. Then, there was the

Directory Service, where I compiled data into computers, ensuring it made its way into the telephone books of each community in BC. Each area had its own set of deadlines.

Things changed a bit down the road when BC Tel merged and became Telus.

As the sands of time passed, my seniority grew, paving the way for me to move up into different jobs, so I went into residential sales and services. Talking to people about their accounts and making changes became my daily task. My last job was in Business Inside Sales, where we sold telephone systems, switchboards, and services to businesses, both big and small.

I worked at BC Telephone / Telus and retired at 60 years of age after 40 years of service.

Right after joining BC Tel, I got my own cozy one-bedroom apartment. On top of working, I decided to take on some night time college courses in biology, chemistry, and mathematics. I stuck with it for a solid four years because I had this big dream of becoming a Naturopath. Sadly, biology wasn't my strong suit, and it was a must-have for my goal. I passed the other subjects, but it broke my heart to let go of that dream.

Dr Earl was retiring, so he referred me to his son. Dr. Kelly Farnsworth has just graduated and has relocated to North Vancouver, B.C. I made an appointment with Dr. Kelly Farnsworth. It had been a while since I had a cranial, and I thought that I should just get checked out. Well, most of the passages were closed. I went three times a week, once a day, for at least a couple of months. I called Dr. Kelly Farnsworth (Dr. Kelly), and he started with three finger cots to start and then increased when needed to about six finger cots until all passages were open. I went back for a few more months, about twice a month, just to make sure everything was stable and in place. I had to return about every three months just to ensure stability. This group of treatments was hard on Dr. Kelly as it had been a while since the last treatment. I had to hold my breath longer until he was able to get through the passage, so he had to use more pressure. We were both exhausted.

I went back to see Dr Kelly when I felt I needed treatments, and with my night school and working and the stress, I was back to regular treatments a few days a week for a few months. After this, I only needed to check in yearly.

Dr. Kelly was just as good as his father, and the elimination of traveling back and forth to Kamloops was a blessing.

While my Naturopath dream faded, I made a solid move at 22 years of age and bought a townhouse in Burnaby, BC. It was the exact one I had my eyes on in my earlier years, though they threw on some shiny aluminum siding. I lived there solo for four years. It was a quiet place, so I decided to start playing the accordion that I loved, and I enrolled in lessons. I was so happy, and now I found something to fill my spare time. And when I was stressed, I could play marches, and when happy, I would play calm music. My life was complete.

Chapter 11

Caring and Bringing Joy to Special People

My grandmother had a soft spot in her heart for me. We are so much alike in so many ways. She was a true Christian; she held Bible studies at her home and at church, taught Sunday school to all ages, and worked as a janitor at the Church they were attending along with her husband. As she was a baker, the word got out, and she started baking pastries for the Timberline Ranch in Maple Ridge, B.C.

I would call her and ask what she was doing, and she said, "Well, I have just made 45 pies, 20 cakes, 15 loaves of bread and 20 dozen cookies." All this was in her small kitchen, and she was getting it ready to take to the guest ranch.

I would ask her if I could join her at church, and she was so happy she could finally show off her granddaughter to others. I would go to Sunday school, join the choir, and take what was like brownies for girls. If she needed help at the church for any function, I would go and help her.

The only thing I did not learn was her baking. She had such a busy life with all that she was doing that there was no time for us to spend a lot of time together. But I have all her cookbooks, and they go back to the late 1900's. That is so special. They had a different way of measuring things out, but just having her cookbooks is great.

As they got older, I would take them to their grocery shopping appointments, and when they could not drive anymore, I would drive them. She enjoyed my husband, Don, and had a special place in her heart for him as well. She always had us over for dinner. My grandfather was always quiet and would not say much. We would all play cards after dinner, and that was good. But just to have grandma's cooking and desserts was the best.

Grandma was always there when you needed her. She made me a bridal quilt when I got married, and I still use it today, 35 years later. It is gorgeous, and it's getting a little thin, but I'm taking care of it.

Don and I were over at her place for dinner and playing cards, and all of a sudden, she could not pick up the cards, and that was not like Grandma.

The next day, we rushed to the doctor for tests, and the results hit us like a ton of bricks: brain cancer. But it wasn't Grandma who got the diagnosis; it was someone else in our family. The doctors scheduled surgery at the Cancer Centre, but shockingly, they told us they wouldn't treat because they thought there were younger patients who needed their help more. We couldn't just accept that, so we reported to the doctor, and he was let go from his job.

Grandma underwent surgery, but unfortunately, the cancer was deep inside her brain, beyond the reach of treatment. Her family doctor allowed her to spend her final days at home, providing pain relief with morphine as needed. She fought bravely for a year, but eventually, her time came.

During that year, my mom and I visited Grandma regularly. When other family members wanted to see her as her health declined, Grandma made it clear that only Mom and I were welcome. She said, "If you couldn't be there for me when I was well, don't come see me when I'm dying." It made me feel incredibly special and cherished to know that she felt that way about me.

After my dad retired he had two heart attacks in 20 minutes which left him paralyzed on the right side from his shoulders to his toes. After trying to learn how to manage to gain use of his right side did not work he found himself in a care home in Burnaby, BC. With no one else available, I took on the responsibility of caring for him for 14 years. Despite the challenges, he remained appreciative. My routine involved visiting him four plus times a week and sharing tea and cookies in the care home—a small but meaningful ritual in our journey together.

His left hand presented another obstacle, complicating eating and drinking. I devoted significant time to encouraging him to use it, even attempting the risky alternative of his less dominant hand. The experiment was short-lived, and we reverted to working on his left hand. Persistence paid off, and with practice, he made remarkable progress.

Observing the loneliness in other residents who went unnoticed, I approached the Care Home with a proposal. Alongside another caregiver, we sought permission to take competent residents, including my dad, on monthly outings using Handydart for lunch or dinner. The success of these outings depended on the assistance I could gather.

We discovered another option, which was to use the music room next to the current dining room, with permission, to set up another dining room area where we would order food. Each participant contributed $10 with the option of what they wanted for dinner. Their options could be, for example, corn on the cob, Chinese food, pizza, etcetera. They were happy as they could eat something they liked that was not provided in the center's provisions.

We even had access to a little kitchen used for family members, so occasionally, we cooked up pork chops or whatever they were in the mood for. It became a cherished ritual, and we spent every penny. This called for a lot of organization, and we did this once a month.

Including in the month's gatherings, any leftover money I purchased and distributed in little gift bags (some things in the bags were chocolates, candy, and little jewelry) were treasured. They eagerly anticipated next month's gathering.

For birthdays, Thanksgiving, Easter, and Xmas, we organized unique dinners, either in the care home's music room or at an external venue. I made it a point to consult the residents on their preferred desserts for the meal that I would make or buy. Their joy was ingratiating. Some would eagerly inquire if we were getting together that month, going so far as to plan unique baths and hair days to ensure they looked and felt their best.

Birthdays and special holidays became grand affairs. Each celebrant got to choose their party menu, and special cakes marked the occasion. During my visits, some residents would approach, asking, "Eileen, when's the next dinner?" These gatherings became a lifeline for seniors, offering something to look forward to and making them feel cherished in a world where not everyone felt welcome. It was more than just meals; it was a connection that added vibrancy to their lives, contributing to their longevity and a sense of being truly special.

We enlisted the music teacher to swing by and play some tunes, and before we knew it, everyone wanted to be part of the action. It was like the floodgates had opened. The music sessions were a hit, the missing piece that brought joy to our gatherings. The tunes took everyone back to the good old days, playing songs from Benny Goodman, Glenn Miller, and Louis Armstrong—the kind of music that resonated with each resident's era.

What started with just six residents turned into a full-blown affair. By the time we decided to wrap things up, we had over 40 residents and even staff joining our dinners. It got to the point where our little get-togethers had more attendees than the regular dining room. It wasn't just about the food anymore; it became a community event, something that brought people together. The music teacher's visits became a highlight, creating a connection through the shared enjoyment of timeless melodies. Our modest dinner gatherings had transformed into lively gatherings, creating a sense of camaraderie that surpassed the confines of our everyday routines.

Juggling my own illness while supporting my friend in her battle against Multiple Sclerosis, a friend I had requested assistance from the onset of this endeavor, made it far from easy. Nevertheless, we couldn't turn a blind eye to the joy we witnessed among the seniors. The routine involved enlisting family members to assist with setting up and taking down tables, arranging place settings, preparing chairs, ordering and fetching food, buying goodie bags, and finally, the cleanup. Taking residents in manual wheelchairs back to their rooms was part of the drill, and finding volunteers wasn't exactly a breeze.

As time passed, recruiting help became a struggle, and the workload became overwhelming for the two of us. It was disheartening because the residents genuinely cherished the events. Bringing a sparkle to their eyes offered something to anticipate and markedly improved the quality of their meals.

The camaraderie, the friendships formed, and witnessing their smiles became my most excellent source of inner joy and a profound sense of purpose. However, we kept this up for four years until the passing of my dad in January 2015.

When my dad was nearing the end of his life, he made a special request: he wanted me to stay with him in his room all the time, day and night. His room was in a care home, and we had to share a hospital bed. It was a tight squeeze because my dad was a big man, six feet tall and 180 pounds, and he was paralyzed on one side. I'm also six feet tall but much lighter at 118 pounds. He would try to make room for me, but it was difficult for him to move.

My dad also apologized after he passed and said he wished he could have done better and please forgive him.

Despite the cramped space, I slept beside him in that bed for a whole week. I couldn't even leave the room when my other siblings came to visit. But on the day he passed away, he didn't want me in the room with him. Later, I learned that it was his way of apologizing for all the difficulties he had put me through. He wanted me to know that he was sorry.

His departure marked a somber day for the residents in our little gathering, now left with nothing to look forward to. Some succumbed to the weight of loneliness and death.

After my father passed, it was now time to look after my Mother. It was a lot easier. My brother looked after her at his house until she had to go into care, and then I took over the reins.

Mom had a hard life as she was in elementary school when she had to stop school and look after her younger brother as her Mom was divorced and was operating a bakery to make ends meet.

Her brother had a better life and ended up finishing school and was eventually a captain on the tug boats going all around the world.

After all the siblings left home my Mother decided to get a job. She took courses at Douglas College to become a Homemaker, looking after seniors in their home and doing their housework, cooking meals, going grocery shopping or just spending time with them. There was one problem though, she never learned how to drive so all her commuting was by bus or taxi's. Mom enjoyed her job and maintained it until she retired.

Mom enjoyed the care facility as she had her own room and got to know some people to talk to. She was having trouble remembering but was able to go out for a walk on her own for a short time. I would come and take her to Dairy Queen banana split, International House of Pancakes, Wendy's for frosty's and hamburgers, and Tim Horton's tea and donuts, which were her favorite as well. My husband Don and Mom's birthday was on the same day, so that was another good reason to go for a banana split. They both enjoyed celebrating their birthdays together at Dairy Queen.

She was a smoker, and it got to the point when dementia sent in; we arranged with the staff that she had to go to the receptionist and get her smokes. It was kind of nice, as she would have just finished a smoke outside and come in and asked for another, and they would say you just had one. Her answer was, "Really, I thought it was at least an hour." It eventually got to the point where she always forgot to go and ask for a smoke, and she eventually quit.

Mom had good care at the facility until she needed a walker and alot more help, and then her health went downhill quickly. I would take her to meals, but she would say she had already eaten and pushed herself away from the table. I said, "Mom, we just got here to have lunch," I just ate. If I had not been there, they would not have had enough staff to ensure everyone was looked after. I complained a lot, but what could be done?

My girlfriend Margaret, who lived close to the care facility, and I would join Mom for tea time or bingo. She loved Margaret coming with me to visit her, and there were many chuckles during the visit.

I tried to help Mom as much as I could to try and reciprocate a little of what she did for me. Just before her passing, I was in her room, and she wanted me to lay on her bed with her and take a selfie of the two of us. She never asked any other sibling to do that. I had a special place in Mom's heart, but she could not express or say it until she passed. Then, one day after she passed, I heard a voice, and it was Mom apologizing for not doing enough for me and the things I had to go through. In my eyes, she did more than I would have ever expected her to do.

I always told Mom that I treasured and was thankful for every day and everything she had to struggle with during my upbringing, which was not easy with more siblings at home.

Mom had very few friends and just wanted the best for her children. She was proud of how we all turned out.

Mom was just a quiet person who always wanted to make others happy and nevermind what she wanted.

I asked Mom one day if she would like to go on a holiday. She said, "That would be ok." Then I asked where she would like to go. She would never suggest anything; I asked her how about going to Nashville to see Charlie Pride. That would be nice. Yeah, got an answer out of her. Then she said, "Memphis is not far from there. Can we go to Graceland?" Great, I will book it.

Well, the day came all packed up, and off we went. Had a great time in Nashville. On the paddlewheeler, tours through the town saw Charlie Pride.

I would bring her over to where I live on the Sunshine Coast, BC semi waterfront, and she loved it. Just sitting on the deck, looking out at the water and relaxing.

My parents had grades three and four and they did their best for what they were handed in life. Throughout it all, I made sure to tell them that I loved them and thanked them for all the sacrifices they had made for me. It was important to me that he knew how much he meant to me, even in his final moments.

I would not change my parents for anyone. They did the best they could.

In this journey, I found a different kind of fulfillment, a calling to help others that surpassed my initial path of becoming a Naturopath. The impact of those years left a lasting impression, shaping my understanding of the profound importance of human connection and the role of compassion in making a difference in people's lives.

Reflecting on my life, I realize I've been blessed with three amazing people: Grandma, my mom, and my dad. Their strength, wisdom, and selflessness have shaped me in profound ways. I'll always hold dear the memories of our time together and the love we shared. I hope I was able to give them the comfort, peace, and love they deserved in their final days. They'll forever hold a special place in my heart.

Chapter 12

Finding Happiness

I was dared to meet someone, and I said I was not interested, but being dared, I thought I would pull the dare.

I put an ad in the Burnaby Now newspaper looking for someone and no luck. I was reading the paper a few weeks later and spotted this ad. It said short, male, 5'2" looking for …. Well, I replied as anyone that puts in short, I knew that I had to meet the challenge. We were soon talking on the phone, and the friendship continued. We decided to meet at Nuffy's Donuts in New Westminster. I told him I was tall, so he arrived there first, anticipating my arrival. Then I came through the door, and he automatically knew it was me as I was the only tall one entering.

We were both shy and not used to talking to people, but somehow, we could feel what each other was going through and talking about our past, and that brought our bond together stronger.

We met in November 1985, got Engaged in February 1986, and married in October 1986. His name is Don. He was from Kamloops and had a son and a daughter. If I was going to settle down, they had to be from Kamloops, as that is where I was always going for treatments, and I wanted a son and daughter or a set of twins.

I was not able to have a family because of being born with Trigonocephaly. My bone structure may not be able to carry a fetus, and also, I was told the following different scenarios: I was told I would live, the fetus would die; we would both die; I would die, the fetus lives, or the fetus could be worse than I was; there was a possible chance of twins as Don was a twin. When he was born, he weighed one pound and a quarter, and his brother was born at one and a half pounds but died at birth. His parents were told things similar to my parents. He would not survive, have breathing issues, and not be able to do a lot of things. So he fought his whole life to prove them wrong. This made our relationship strong as we had to fight for our lives.

It was hard for me to be around other babies or younger children. I thought I had a family when I married Don, but I found out that the Mother was abusing the children. That broke our hearts to see the children being abused by Mom, and because we were working, the Court system prevented us from getting custody of them.

Don did not struggle as much as I did medically, but he had his challenges in life and school. He always tried to prove others wrong and that he could do whatever he put his mind to.

Chapter 13

Life Together

After we were married, Don joined me in the townhouse, and we made it our home for three years.

In my mind, the destination was crystal clear. It was a vision that had taken root long ago, even before the decision to bid farewell to the townhouse. Driving through the streets of Port Coquitlam, we passed by a house that had always occupied a special place in my dreams – a house I had earmarked as my future haven.

Weeks rolled by, each filled with anticipation as we scoured the market for potential homes. Then, like a beacon calling us home, the house of my dreams appeared on the market. It stood head and shoulders above the rest, boasting features that captured our hearts. Without hesitation, we claimed it as our own.

This charming abode had a lot to offer. A cozy 2-bedroom basement suite adorned with a rustic wood-burning fireplace welcomed tenants throughout our ownership. We set out to infuse our personal touch in renovations that transformed the space into an extension of our identity. The subterranean realm housed a spacious living area, a bathroom with a shower, a dining room, and a kitchen.

Venturing upstairs, we discovered the soul of our home. Original hardwood floors cradled our footsteps, guiding us through three bedrooms, a 3-piece bathroom with a tub and shower, linen and coat closets, and another captivating wood-burning fireplace. The expansive living room and a well-appointed kitchen seamlessly melded into a dining area, creating a perfect backdrop for countless memories. Nestled on nearly a double lot, encircled by a protective fence, and crowned with a carport that we lovingly transformed into a garage, our new haven promised both comfort and space.

For 26 years, we reveled in the joys of living on the upper floor while the basement played host to contented tenants. A harmonious existence unfolded, marked by the warmth of our hearth and the quiet companionship of a good tenant. Our home, a canvas of experiences, reflected the love and care we poured into every nook and cranny.

Our cocker spaniel, Bailey, wasn't exactly a fan of the yard. He had a habit of barking up a storm, so most of the time, he preferred the cozy confines of the house.

Don was having problems with breathing and coughing, so he went to the Doctor, and she made an appointment with the Respirologist. Bad news: diagnosed with COPD. The doctor said she would monitor and do testing to see what tool would be good for him to help with his breathing. He was eventually put onto a CPAP machine that would help him with breathing at night.

Chapter 14
A Battle With Chronic Pain

After I experienced several injurious car accidents, the cumulative toll on my health became apparent.

Following each accident, increasing numbness in my right arm prompted me to seek various treatments, from physiotherapy to acupuncture, without significant relief. The condition eventually interfered with my ability to work. Seeking answers, I consulted my doctor, leading to a diagnosis of Chronic Regional Pain Syndrome (CRPS). The specialist recommended nerve blocks, and I underwent 12 procedures, each inserting permanent freezing into a sympathetic nerve in my neck. Unfortunately, the relief was short-lived, lasting only about 20 minutes before my arm reverted to its numb and useless state.

Frustrated by the limited success of nerve blocks, the specialist proposed surgery – a sympathectomy. He went in and collapsed the lung and then proceeded to go to the sympathetic nerve located near the second or third lumbar vertebra and cut it. This procedure took place in December 1999, resulting in an unexpected turn of events. Instead of improving, the CRPS now had spread throughout my entire body. Disheartened, I returned to the specialist, who admitted that the surgery should not have been performed as it had been 25 years since the first symptoms occurred, given the duration of my condition. It was a disheartening revelation.

Now, instead of a limp right arm, I contend with CRPS affecting my entire body. The pain and numbness intensify with changes in barometric pressure and exposure to elements such as wind, sun, rain, heat, cold, air conditioning, or a breeze. The sensation of my body burning up is accompanied by excruciating pain, creating a daily struggle.

The journey through the maze of medical interventions took a toll on my body. The doctors prescribed gabapentin, a medication that caused a weight gain of 30 pounds. Despite reaching an unheard-of dosage of 2800 mg per day just to remain at work, my condition deteriorated. The constant exposure to air conditioning became unbearable, making simple tasks like typing and walking excruciatingly difficult. My body rebelled against the keyboard, leaving my arms useless, and I clung to chairs and tables just to shuffle to the bathroom.

Then, the breaking point hit. I mustered the strength to drive to work one last time, but the car door became an insurmountable barrier. That marked the end of my career.

Returning to my specialist, I was switched to Lyrica, hoping for a better outcome. However, this shift came with its own set of challenges. I endured three months of relentless coughing, only to discover that Lyrica had damaged my chest wall muscles, resulting in Bronchiectasis. This chronic condition is a long-term condition where the airways of the lungs become widened, leading to a buildup of excess mucus that can make the lungs more vulnerable to infection. The most common symptom includes a persistent cough that usually brings up phlegm and shortness of breath.

Transitioning to Effexor proved to be a more suitable solution, free from the adverse effects of previous medications. Despite this improvement, the relentless grip of air conditioning prevented my return to work. At the age of 46, I found myself on short-term disability, eventually transitioning to long-term disability for life.

I continued seeing Dr. Kelly Farnsworth for treatments, initially requiring sessions once or twice a year. These sessions spanned one to two days a week for three months until my passages stabilized. Over time, the intervals between treatments extended to every three to four years, contingent on my stress levels. I witnessed a remarkable change – my peaked forehead flattened for the first time, albeit temporarily.

Chapter 15

Finding Our Retirement Home

I had this idea of finding a perfect place for our retirement, so I suggested to my husband that we should start exploring. We got in touch with a Real Estate Agency and asked them to scout out some houses in Sechelt for us. A realtor called one day and said, " I've found some places in Sechelt, so let's meet up." We were thrilled and agreed to head over on the weekend. The anticipation was real; we couldn't wait for the weekend adventure.

I chose Sechelt as I went there when I was little camping with my family and enjoyed it, so I thought I would come back and check it out again.

Finally, the weekend arrived. We hopped on our Harley Davidson motorcycle and made our way to the ferry terminal in Horseshoe Bay, Vancouver. Our plan was to catch the ferry to Langdale, Gibsons, and then head to Sechelt. As we chatted with folks in line, the ferry rolled in, and we excitedly boarded. But then, the captain's voice came over the speakers, "Welcome to the Queen of Surrey to Nanaimo." Wait, what? Panic set in.

Don went straight to the captain and said, "We need to go to Langdale. Can you turn the ferry around?" The captain, calm as can be, replied, "Stay on board. When we go back to Horseshoe Bay, you can catch the ferry to Langdale." Relieved, we agreed and thanked the captain. Later, we found out that the people we were chatting with were BC Ferry employees. If only we'd asked them earlier if we were in the right line!

Well, it turned out alright. Since we were on the Harley, it was no big deal to turn the bike around on the ferry. We even took a shortcut to catch the Langdale Ferry. The sun was shining, making it a lovely day to just enjoy the ride. Despite the unexpected detour, our excitement to start exploring properties for our retirement was stronger than ever.

So, we finally made it to Sechelt and met up with the realtor, who handed us the current listings, saying, "Go check them out and let me know if you like any." Off we went, driving around, exploring one place after another, but nothing quite caught our fancy. That is until we stumbled upon the last one.

After cruising down a dead-end road, there it was—the last house. And, oh boy, did it have a view! I couldn't help but exclaim, "Wow, this view is something else! You can see straight up the inlet; it's semi-waterfront, and no one can build in front of us to ruin this perfect view." I turned to Don and said, "If this place has a fireplace, we're buying it."

It was already occupied, though. It turns out that a realtor was crashing there temporarily after his rental place burned down. We couldn't help but ask, "Is this cabin still up for grabs?" To our delight, he said, "Yes, it is." We were "over the moon," stumbling upon this dream home.

Eager to take a peek, we asked if we could look around. The realtor, generous as can be, said, "By all means." And there it was—a cozy little cabin with a workshop and an electric furnace in the quarter basement, a carport with the hot water tank tucked underneath, and the electric breaker box sitting outside in the carport but nice and dry. Upstairs, three bedrooms with just one closet, a full kitchen boasting a half wood and half electric stove, and a three-piece bathroom with a shower only. The cherry on top was a tiny living room with a brick fireplace!

Thrilled doesn't quite cover it. A fully furnished 500-square-foot Lynden home with an unbelievable view, semi waterfront with no one to block our view of the wide open ocean inlet, all for $40,000. We didn't waste a second—bought it on the spot. Both of us were ecstatic. It was our first joint purchase, and what a way to kick off our journey together.

After years of back-and-forths to Sechelt and family visits, we stumbled upon a delightful twist of fate – it turns out we used to camp on the very property we now proudly owned, long before any homes dotted the landscape. And to add to the serendipity, my dad had worked in logging camps all through the inlets, making him intimately familiar with the area. It felt like the universe had guided us here, connecting the dots between our past and our present.

Weekends in the cabin became our cherished escape. We'd unwind, clean up the property that had been a bit neglected, and revel in the simple joy of being there.

One exciting new adventure was taking our 12-foot aluminum boat out for crabbing. It was a first for us, and dropping the crab trap, tying it to a buoy that served as an anchor, and coming back hours later to a full trap became our routine. Sorting through the catch, we'd release the ones that didn't meet the criteria and keep only what we could. Don couldn't help but express, "This is so relaxing and enjoyable." We'd also take our cocker spaniel, Bailey, out for boat tours around the inlet. He'd find a cool spot on the aluminum floor and doze off.

As the sun bothered me, I asked Don, "Can you get a canopy for the boat so that I can stay out longer?" He promised to look into it, and the next time we ventured out, there it was – the canopy. I expressed my gratitude, "Now we can relax on the water for a long time."

On rainy days, the sound of raindrops tapping on the roof and the occasional visit from birds and squirrels became a calming symphony for us. Don would often remark, "It's so relaxing just hearing that noise."

The air in Sechelt was so crisp and fresh that an afternoon nap became a daily ritual – something quite unusual for us. We'd joke, "All we seem to do when we're here is sleep." The relaxed atmosphere left us with little motivation to do anything else.

I was hesitant to rent the cabin. But then, a ray of hope appeared. Friends of ours, Rick and Ann, expressed interest in renting. Their request brought a sense of relief, and I thought, "They'll be good tenants." I agreed, "Okay, that would make me very happy to have good tenants." Rick and Ann became occupants, and they proved to be wonderful tenants. They stayed for a total of 10 years, with no issues and a great relationship with the neighbors. I told Don, "I'm glad we finally have good tenants. They'll improve the cabin instead of wrecking it." Don agreed, "Yes, they will be good." It was a much-needed turnaround for our cabin and our faith in renters.

Chapter 16

Unexpected Change of Events

One day, a phone call from our friend Rick jolted us from our routine. His voice trembled as he shared the news, "A massive 150-foot, 30-ton fir tree just came crashing down onto the cabin in Sechelt." My immediate response was to tell him, "Keep me posted on what's happening, and I'll be over first thing in the morning." My hands shook, and shock coursed through me. All I could think about was the daunting task of dealing with the aftermath.

Rick, still reeling from the shock, recounted the close call. Just a week before, he had moved into the larger bedroom. That fateful night, he found himself in the living room when the lights began to flicker. Heading to the kitchen for a flashlight, he decided to turn it in for the night in case the power went out. Little did he know, a colossal tree was about to rewrite the narrative of his home.

Miraculously, the tree narrowly missed his bedroom. Instead, it found its mark in the adjacent room, landing just above his collection of chainsaws. Its destructive path carved through the cabin, starting from the corner of the living room straight through to the bedroom. Astonishingly, the kitchen, bathroom, and his bedroom escaped unscathed.

What made the situation even more surreal was that Rick's German Shepherd wasn't in the house that day – a deviation from the norm. In the midst of the chaos, I found solace in the fact that no one was hurt or lost their life. Gratitude welled up as Rick shared that the flickering lights had served as an eerie prelude, giving him a crucial heads-up.

Remarkably, the house shifted about four feet to the left, and yet, amidst the upheaval, not a single item was damaged or lost. Once the colossal tree was removed, a sense of relief washed over us. Rick was able to recover all his possessions, including earplugs and jewelry. The fact that the Lyndal home came in two pieces turned out to be a saving grace, as it separated into two parts, sparing some of the most cherished corners of his abode. In the face of such unpredictability, we couldn't help but count our blessings and acknowledge the silver lining in a situation that could have taken a much darker turn.

In the midst of the chaos, Rick's voice cut through the tension, a mix of relief and happiness, "I'm so glad all my stuff made it through unscathed." I couldn't help but echo his sentiment, "Yeah, I'm really grateful too."

As we surveyed the aftermath, the miracle was clear – all the walls stood tall, and not a single window had succumbed to the tree's wrath, except the one Rick had to break to re-enter the house. It was a scene of resilience, almost surreal in its intactness.

Rick, with a fire flickering in the free-standing fireplace, had to act swiftly. The tree's impact on the stove caused the chimney to unravel, but miraculously, it all landed outside without a single ash escaping. The neighbors, quick on their feet, dialed up the fire department. Their swift response was crucial in a neighborhood surrounded by trees, potential kindling for a disastrous fire. The fireplace, once a centerpiece, now resembled the aftermath of a football game – smashed but, against all odds, not a catalyst for widespread destruction. The firefighters marveled, "It's a wonder it didn't set the trees ablaze or cause any injuries."

In a surreal twist, the microwave, perched on a tilted shelf above the stove, defied gravity and stayed put. While the tree refrained from invading the kitchen, a mysterious force shattered the glass in the oven door, leaving us scratching our heads in bewilderment.

Venturing around the side of the house, I couldn't contain my amazement. "Come check this out," I shouted, pointing to the woodpile that had once snugly hugged the house, now miraculously relocated four feet away, with not a single piece of wood out of place. It was a collective moment of astonishment.

The house, though shifted, clung steadfast to its foundation, defying the odds. "It's incredible," I remarked. "Someone up there must be looking out for us." In the aftermath of nature's fury, the threads of luck and protection woven into the fabric of our experience were undeniable. Gratitude filled the air as we marveled at the inexplicable series of events that spared not only our belongings but also our home and, most importantly, our well-being.

As we navigated the aftermath, the insurance wheels were set in motion, summoning a crew to whisk away the remnants of the fallen giant. A stern voice advised, "You've got to cut down all these trees to prevent a repeat performance." My response? "No problem, at least we'll have firewood for ages." Amidst the practical considerations, a twinge of sadness crept in when I asked, "Can I at least keep a piece of the wood as a memento?" The answer came, matter-of-factly, "Sure, if you want to dodge the insurance claim." The decision was a no-brainer – $200k trumped sentimental wood.

Chapter 17

The Bad News

While I was in Sechelt, grappling with the sight of our battered cabin, the phone rang, and Don's daughter, Tanya's voice carried urgent news, "Dad's health is taking a turn for the worse. You've got to come home." Without a second thought, I found myself on the ferry that very afternoon. Don's persistent cough echoed in my ears, a stark reminder of his defiance against medical advice – he was still smoking despite being told to quit. My constant refrain echoed through our conversations, "If you really want to retire, you've got to kick the smoking habit. It's not happening if you keep it up." The urgency of the situation hung heavy in the air, weaving together the threads of both personal and property challenges in a tapestry of life's unpredictability.

When Don's persistent cough escalated to a point where he couldn't catch his breath, he remained steadfast in downplaying the severity. Convinced that smoking wasn't the culprit, he brushed off the signs of distress. It reached a breaking point, a moment when the incessant coughing and breathlessness became too much to ignore. I arrived home, looked at him, and declared, "We need to call an ambulance. You're not okay." His response was a feeble moan, insisting, "I'm fine." My counter, firm and unwavering, echoed through the tension-filled air, "Either I take you by car or the ambulance, but you're going. You are not good."

The weight of stress bore down on me as I insisted on heading to the hospital. The ambulance whisked him away, and in the emergency room, the situation turned dire. Don flatlined twice, sending shockwaves through an already overwhelmed reality. Swiftly, they transferred him to intensive care once he stabilized. There, a nurse stood vigil by his side 24/7, monitoring every fluctuation in his delicate state for two agonizing months.

In the midst of the chaos, my world became a haze of stress and tears. Fumbling through the unknown, I reached out to Don's brother, one of 10 siblings, in Kamloops, my voice cracking as I uttered, "Don is in emergency intensive care, and we don't know his condition." His brother, sensing the gravity, assured me, "I'm leaving Kamloops and will be there as soon as I can."

The family rallied from different corners — his son from Manitoba, sisters from Alberta, and others from Kamloops and the mainland. In the hospital corridors, I gathered them and delivered the heartbreaking news, "He's only allowed two people at once; he's not doing well." Their shock mirrored my own as they whispered, "Seeing him like this is not fair." I offered solace, "I'll be here and keep you all informed when you leave. I understand you can't stay long, but thank you for coming to pay your respects. Don appreciates it."

After an emotional gathering, we sought refuge at IHOP for lunch. Amidst the clatter of cutlery and plates, we grappled with the harsh reality, discussing Don's condition, our stress palpable, and tears freely flowing. In those moments, the fragility of life hung in the air, and our collective strength became a lifeline, grounding us in the face of uncertainty.

As Don's battle with COPD unfolded, the toll on his body was evident – he shed about 20 pounds during his hospital stay. Despite the weight loss, he seemed to rally, a deceptive appearance that masked the gradual worsening of his condition over time. The diagnosis marked the beginning of a relentless decline, necessitating the introduction of medical interventions. Post-hospitalization, the CPAP machine, portable oxygen, and eventually a 24/7 reliance on oxygen became integral to his daily routine. The root cause is traced back to the compromised lung muscles, a consequence of his premature birth. Navigating this tumultuous journey together, both of us were enveloped in stress, unsure of what lay ahead. I looked at Don and said, "I don't want you to leave me. You'll be okay."

Thank goodness it was time for another cranial, and yes, I knew I had some closed passages as my temper was getting out of control, which showed a cranial was needed. I went to Dr. Kelly, and only a few passages were closed, and I felt better after the treatment. It was nice to find the treatments are now moving farther apart and are only sparked on by stress. So I just had to try to control my stress level, and everything will be good. Oh, Good Luck! I would go back in six months to see how things are.

Chapter 18

Designing Spaces And Building Bonds

Seeking a supportive environment, I brought our motorhome that we had purchased a few months ago to Sechelt, settling it at Bayside Campground and RV Park for a year. Nestled on the route to our new home, the site offered not only a peaceful retreat but also the comfort of nearby neighbors. That support proved invaluable one snowy morning when I found the weight of snow burdening the awning. Contemplating how to remove it without causing damage, I improvised with a broom handle, banging away from the underside. Just as I wrestled with the task, my neighbor Brad appeared. Curious, he asked, "What are you doing?" I explained, "Trying to get the snow off the awning." Without hesitation, Brad insisted, "I'll help. Go inside and stay warm." Grateful, I retreated, and within minutes, Brad had resolved the issue. Expressing my appreciation, I shared how fortunate I felt to have him as a neighbor.

In an attempt to reciprocate the kindness, I started baking cookies and muffins, delivering some to Brad, who lived alone. He appreciated the gesture, and during one of our exchanges, I asked, "What brings you to Sechelt?" His reply offered insight, "My family is in Powell River, and I work for BC Hydro. They stationed me here for a year to help out." In those moments, the RV park transformed into more than a temporary abode; it became a community where mutual support and simple acts of kindness made the challenges a bit more bearable.

I found myself in the unexpected role of contractor, overseeing a process that was entirely new to me. The excitement bubbled within as I navigated the intricacies of hiring subcontractors and immersing myself in the construction journey.

The first order of business was clearing the property of all trees, a necessary step to meet insurance requirements and safeguard our new haven from potential arboreal threats. Though it stung a bit to witness the once-forested backyard transformed into a barren landscape, I consoled myself with the thought that safety trumped aesthetics. The fallen tree, a relic of the past, became a source of warmth for four winters, chopped up for firewood. The rest of the wood found a new purpose at a portable sawmill in Halfmoon Bay.

The literal groundwork began with digging a hole for the house – a task that unfolded into a sizable excavation. Returning to the property after a bout of rain, I was greeted by an unexpected yet delightful sight – ducks gracefully paddling in the newly formed hole. Nature, it seemed, was eager to leave its mark on our construction journey.

In the realm of builders, I brought on Bill to lead the charge, only to discover that he enlisted the help of his son, Justin, and a friend named Paul. Initially, I wrestled with the idea of entrusting our dream to a couple of guys in their twenties. However, their qualifications and dedication quickly put my concerns to rest. I adopted the role of a daily inspector, ensuring that the progress aligned with our vision. The goal was to have everything locked up – framed, finished roof in place, walls ready for siding, plumbing, electrical, doors, windows, and septic all installed. Despite the initial reservations, I chose to let their expertise guide the construction, laying the foundation for a home that would encapsulate our dreams and stand as a testament to the journey we were undertaking.

Bringing my roofer buddy, Henry, all the way from Port Coquitlam to lay down the shingles was just the beginning. Next up, I roped in a professional gutter company while Justin and Paul tackled the crucial task of installing the flashing. Now, it was my turn to roll up my sleeves and dive into the real nitty-gritty. Let the work commence!

Justin and Paul, the dynamic duo in their twenties, got the ball rolling by constructing five sturdy frames from two-by-twelves, each measuring a robust 12 feet by 12 feet. They cleverly added rows across, creating a convenient setup for me to slap on cedar siding and pine. Efficiency was the name of the game – stain multiple boards at once. Once the first frame was brimming with freshly stained wood, I stacked another one on top, and the rhythm continued until all five frames were teeming with potential.

As the boards dried, I plucked them off the top frame for round two of the stain treatment. It was a well-practiced dance, repeating the process until each piece of cedar and pine was bathed in a rich, protective hue. The third round brought a twist – flipping the boards over for a single coat on the opposite side before stacking them one last time. The efficiency was staggering, a quick-paced ballet of staining that left me both impressed and, I must admit, thoroughly exhausted. The weather was on our side throughout this undertaking, but by the end, I declared a temporary truce with all things stain-related. I needed a breather.

Justin and Paul, ever the helpful duo, sensing my weariness, chimed in, "Hey, we can handle the staining for you." Their offer was genuine, but my response was resolute, "I enjoy it, and besides, you guys have more important tasks on your plate." They were a tad disappointed they couldn't take over, but in that moment, the camaraderie and shared workload painted a vivid picture of our collaborative effort to turn a mere structure into a warm, stained masterpiece, a standing testament to the collective dedication poured into building our dream home.

Curiosity led me to question the people at Rona about the rationale behind applying two coats on one side and just one on the other. Their explanation was straightforward – the double dose on the underside served as a moisture deterrent, preventing any unwanted infiltration, while a single coat on the exterior sufficed. This is another nugget of wisdom to add to my growing collection of construction know-how.

Expressing gratitude for this handy trick, I acknowledged that without it, staining everything would have been an endless task. Their response caught me off guard, "I've never had anyone, especially a woman, help in building their home." My retort? "I enjoy the challenge and the learning experience." It seemed they were anticipating snagging the staining gig, but my enthusiasm and readiness for hands-on work surprised them.

The cedar destined for the exterior received a soothing baby blue stain, a choice influenced by my dad's keen eye. Meanwhile, the pine, meant for the interior, was bathed in a warm cedar hue. Little did I know this seemingly arbitrary decision would result in each room boasting a different shade – a delightful surprise that added a touch of spontaneity to the overall design.

A humorous hiccup surfaced when I went to grab the last can of stain. The clerk, with a perplexed expression, inquired, "What are you using this for?" My matter-of-fact response was, "I'm staining the inside of my house." Their eyebrows shot up as they informed me, "This is for outside wood, not inside." My comeback? "Thanks, but it's a bit too late to change now." In the grand scheme of things, this unintentional mix-up added a layer of uniqueness to our home, a testament to the unforeseen twists and turns that shaped its character.

With the exterior cedar in place, it was my turn to step up to the plate and stain the shingles for the peaks of the house. Drawing from the efficient procedure used before, the process was both effective and speedy, ensuring a uniform and appealing finish.

Moving indoors, the kitchen walls, bathrooms, mechanical and freezer rooms were exempt from the pine treatment, requiring only good old drywall. When the time came to introduce the pine, the tongue-and-groove design made installation a breeze. Each piece was slotted snugly into place and secured with a nail gun, creating a seamless and visually pleasing result. To enhance both support and aesthetics, I staggered each piece, a small touch that made a big difference. The whole process, facilitated by a chop-off saw for precision, unfolded with surprising speed.

Barb lent a hand, contributing to the installation in the laundry, pantry room, and the expansive downstairs bedroom. Upon completion, I pointed out the artistic unintentional pattern – "Two boards light, four boards a bit darker, then two lights." Barb was visibly impressed by the unplanned yet appealing visual effect.

Don, taking pride in his contribution, joined forces with me to install the pine in our bedroom, inside the basement, and beneath the deck. Wrestling with warped wood, we faced a challenge, but determination won the day. Despite the hurdles, Don's sense of accomplishment shone through.

For the trickier ceilings and higher walls, I enlisted the help of my friend Mike. The pine, having weathered the elements, posed a challenge due to warping, but with teamwork and perseverance, we conquered the task.

Delighted with the outcome, I asked Mike for his opinion on the transformed look. His surprised response spoke volumes, "It looks so nice and warm and fresh – much better than painting every room." A sentiment I wholeheartedly agreed with.

Justin and Paul, completing the pinnacle of the project, seamlessly installed the pine and shingles on the peaks of the roof, bringing the culmination of our collective efforts to a visually stunning conclusion.

Engaging in the insulating process was a hands-on endeavor that took me into the nooks and crannies of our future home. I diligently contributed to placing insulation in the walls of the bedrooms upstairs, ensuring the bathrooms received their due layer, and even slipping insulation beneath the tub to thwart any potential heat loss. Little did I know this venture would unveil an unexpected twist.

Amidst the insulation work, a realization struck like a bolt of lightning – one of the bedrooms was amiss. It was smaller than intended and, to add to the oversight, lacked a closet. The frustration bubbled up within me, and I had no one to blame but myself. The revelation stung, and I couldn't help but attribute it to the tensions that simmered on the construction front. I had been relentless in pushing for efficiency, calling out extended breaks, lax work habits, and inconsistent schedules during my weekly meetings with Bill. This, it seemed, was their way of responding, a subtle retaliation through intentional mistakes. Despite the setbacks, I managed to catch most of them before they escalated.

In an effort to rectify the situation, I brought in a professional insulation company to tackle the downstairs area. They skillfully sprayed insulation where the cement retaining walls met the wood frame, ensuring a seamless barrier against the elements. I couldn't help but express my observation to the insulator, "These walls look too snuggly; there's a lot of insulation in them." His response was a snicker and a reassuring statement, "You'll have no problems with heat loss when I get done." Grateful for his expertise and thoughtfulness, I thanked him as a layer of comfort settled over the prospect of a well-insulated home.

I stumbled upon a hidden gem at the Restore in Burnaby – wallpaper adorned with seashells and starfish, priced at a mere twenty-five cents a roll. Eager to infuse a touch of the ocean into our spaces, I wallpapered two walls in both bathrooms, creating a serene atmosphere. In the kitchen, a lively splash of paint adorned the remaining walls.

Attempting to master the art of plastering gyprock in the bathrooms and kitchen proved to be a trickier task than anticipated. My attempts to achieve smooth walls fell short, compelling me to seek professional help. A hired hand stepped in to bring finesse to the bathroom and kitchen walls. The challenge continued as I endeavored to construct a pony wall to partially separate the toilet from the shower. Jack, the tile guy, delivered a reality check, humorously noting, "It looks like a baby pony wall," A pony wall is a half-height sturdy wall. I also built a baby pony wall, but it was not sturdy. His expertise transformed the wobbly structure into a solid and smooth partition.

Venturing into the realm of heating solutions, I took charge of installing a wood-burning stove, serving as both a source of warmth and charm. Bill's initial plan for the fireplace, facing straight along the wall, left room for improvement. Upon noticing a heat register in an awkward spot, I questioned the choice. "Why is there a heat register here? You can't shut it off completely. Why not use the right tool?" Bill admitted to opting for a cheaper alternative. Unwilling to compromise, I took matters into my own hands and procured the correct piece. The fireplace underwent a transformation, now positioned in the corner facing the middle of the living room, with the appropriate vent installed. Bill, acknowledging the improvement, remarked, "Oh, yes, I agree. It looks much better now." This hands-on approach ensured that our living space not only radiated warmth but also reflected thoughtful design choices.

Navigating the world of home improvement led me to a fireplace store with a crucial inquiry, "I need some tile for the floor under and in front of the fireplace. What do you recommend?" The attentive staff showcased a tile that harmonized seamlessly with our color scheme. Enthusiastically, I scheduled an appointment for them to install the fireplace and the chosen tile.

The initial installation was a success, and everything appeared flawless. However, a few weeks down the line, the tile began to betray its promise and started breaking. Frustrated but determined, I returned to the store, seeking answers. The staff, equally puzzled, offered to replace the tile, suspecting it might be faulty. Appreciating their commitment, I agreed. Yet, a few months later, the issue resurfaced. My dissatisfaction was palpable as I made my way back to the store. This time, I suggested a call to the manufacturer for clarity. Lo and behold, it was revealed that the tile was meant solely for wall decoration. Disappointed and feeling a bit let down, I requested a full refund, expressing my dismay at the lack of awareness.

Undeterred, I went on a mission with Don to a flooring store in Sechelt. The revelation that they had a warehouse stocked with discontinued and overstock flooring and tiles proved to be a game-changer. There, we found a suitable tile and had it installed. Not only did it rectify the issue, but it also enhanced the overall aesthetic.

Eager to challenge expectations, I embraced the tools of the trade with gusto. Operating a chainsaw to carve out a window in the wall, wielding a chop-off saw for cutting pine, cedar, and shingles, and confidently using a drill and nail gun for wood installation became my daily routine. It was a thrilling experience, proving to the workers and, more importantly, to myself that I was unafraid and capable of tackling any task that came my way.

Before the completion of the interior stairs, plans called for a towering wall that would stretch from floor to ceiling, acting as a partition between the upstairs and downstairs spaces. Seizing the opportunity to optimize the layout, I proposed a modification to Bill. Rather than a solid barrier, I suggested a four-foot-tall, 12-foot-long wall, a change that was met with agreement and approval from the team.

As the construction of the wall progressed, Bill encountered challenges in ensuring its sturdiness. Drawing from a bit of construction wisdom, I suggested the use of a metal strip nailed from the floor joist to the stud every three feet. To everyone's surprise, especially Bill's, this simple solution proved effective and resolved the stability issues.

Turning attention to the interior stairs, I sourced solid maple treads and sought out someone skilled to install and stain them. Enter David from D. Petersen Furniture Restoration in Sechelt, BC. Discussing the intricacies of maple treads and their finishing, David proposed a solution that caught my interest. "I can stain them in a way that you'll never have to do it again," he assured, presenting a sample of the stain color. Eager for a low-maintenance solution, I agreed, and the final outcome left me delighted with the decision.

In my quest for the perfect stair installation, I found myself interviewing five stair installers, each claiming expertise in their craft. Unfortunately, none seemed to grasp the concept of a flawless installation. Frustration mounted as they all echoed the same approach: "Drill screw holes from the top, secure them downward, and conceal them with plugs."

It wasn't until I stumbled upon Kurt, an Australian carpenter boasting 30 years of experience, that I thought my search had finally ended. Eagerly, I asked him, "Kurt, how would you install the stairs?" Much to my dismay, his response mirrored that of the previous installers. Anger bubbled within me as I retorted, "No! I want them screwed from underneath, leaving no marks on the surface." It was disheartening to realize I had to explicitly convey this preference.

As Kurt set to work on the installation, I closely observed his every move. Plywood covered the risers, stained treads descended, and screws were driven in from below. Yet, my discerning eye caught a flaw – the need for additional security. I pointed out the necessity of a bracket for reinforcement, to which Kurt, seemingly cooperative, said, "I'll get the brackets." However, his choice proved incorrect. Taking matters into my own hands, I located the correct brackets, ensuring a secure fit. Thirty years of experience, it seemed, did not guarantee perfection.

My disappointment deepened when Kurt, despite his claimed expertise, left significant nicks on the stairs and marked the walls. Despite my photographic evidence, he vehemently denied any wrongdoing.

Turning to Bravo Floors & Decor Inc. in Sechelt, BC, I discovered a solution for the flooring problem. Opting for a durable vinyl plank with a wood-like appearance, they expertly installed it in the bedrooms, living room, and kitchen. The bathroom upstairs and the back porch received matching vinyl plank tiles, while the downstairs bathroom boasted ceramic tiles. This was the only company that worked professionally, and I was very satisfied with the outcome. It's nice to know that there are some reliable companies out there that you do not have to babysit. The result? A visually stunning and resilient floor, compensating for the trials and tribulations of the stair installation ordeal.

As I reflected on the journey of building our house, a wave of disbelief washed over me. Despite my sense of pride, the builders questioned my involvement. I had prior knowledge of helping my father build our family home while I was in Junior High School in Quesnel, B.C.

I knew from the amount of stress I was going through that it was time for a cranial, so off I went, and I was right. Not all the passages were closed. I think we caught them in time. I just needed a few balloons to ensure everything was holding firm, and I was told to come back in six months. I was happy that my system was accepting the treatments.

When the time came to construct the back porch and stairs, I reached out to a man named Graham, who had a portable sawmill and had been hired to be responsible for the safekeeping of the trees that were taken off the property, as well as the tree that fell on the house for assistance. "Could you cut me this list of wood for my porch and stairs?" I inquired. Without hesitation, he assured me, "Certainly, and I can deliver it in a week."

However, complications arose when Bill insisted on six-foot-wide stairs, contrary to my preference for four feet. Additionally, he advocated for a trap door in the porch floor to create storage space beneath, a suggestion I vehemently opposed. Despite my objections, Bill stood firm. Frustrated, I declared, "I will get someone else to do the porch and stairs." It was a surprising turn of events.

I enlisted the help of my friend, Thomas, who skillfully crafted four-foot-wide stairs and a delightful porch according to my specifications. Now, I could comfortably walk from the ground beneath the stairs and porch.

Graham later suggested, "You can get money for the wood you have here. We should talk about how much there is here." Surprisingly, the wood had been sitting there for three years without any mention of compensation. However, this conversation took an unexpected turn when I read of his passing in the Coast Reporter a few weeks later.

Regarding the installation of the septic tank, I entrusted Bryce with the task. Unfortunately, a twist of fate occurred when the tank was left temporarily in a hole, filled up with rainwater, and twisted. Panicked, I contacted Bryce, who promptly rectified the situation by digging a new hole for a replacement.

Although relieved that the septic tank issue was resolved, I found myself dismayed as the new hole occupied the middle of my backyard. Expressing my concern to Bryce, I asked if there was an alternative location. Regrettably, he responded, "No, I can't put it back along the fence where the other one was." Resigned to the situation, I reluctantly accepted the placement, acknowledging that sometimes compromises are inevitable when building a home.

Once everything was installed, I couldn't help but question, "Why is the tank so big? Oh, this is the size you need, 1250 liters." Later, I discovered I should have opted for a 650-720-liter tank. Well, at least now I only need it emptied every five years.

Choosing all the appliances, fixtures, vanities, tub, and shower for the house was a task that fell on my shoulders, as Don was unwell. When he eventually made it to Sechelt after the house was complete, he expressed pride in the finished project, marveling at the fact that I had undertaken most of the work.

Our two-story home boasts an upstairs bedroom featuring two side-by-side closets, a den, and a bathroom with a spacious six-foot bathtub. It's a relief to finally stretch out and relax, free from the confines of cramped spaces. Upstairs also houses an accessible toilet (slightly elevated), a living room, a kitchen, a pantry, a laundry area, and a linen closet.

On the lower level, a large bedroom with two side-by-side closets, a washroom featuring a two-seated walk-in shower, another accessible toilet, a freezer/pantry room, a mechanical room for storage, two hot water tanks, and an electrical box. The entrance welcomes two large closets, and an open recreation area completes the downstairs layout.

During Gary's plumbing installation, I was surprised to find two hot water tanks. Inquiring about the reason behind this, he chuckled, "Well, I only connect one to hydro, and the water comes into the second tank that is not connected. By the time the first tank calls for water, it's at room temperature, so you always have hot water on demand." I was rendered speechless but grateful for his foresight in installing two tanks.

Next on the agenda were the kitchen cupboards and the Island. A business card at Bravo Floors led me to Trish, a cabinet maker. In a busy season of construction, I met her at her office, outlined my preferences, and perused samples. Subsequent meetings at the house solidified the plan. Despite Trish's constant reassurances that they were working on a substantial project and I needed to wait, I discovered it was a massive condo development in Sechelt. Despite my growing impatience over the six-month wait and no other reliable options, I held out.

Finally, the day arrived, bringing both excitement and disappointment. The cupboards went up, but the glass in the display cabinet was too small, and they were unwilling to rectify the issue. Then came the counters, intended to be made of Corian, a low-maintenance material.

Upon closer inspection, dissatisfaction crept in as I noticed some doors were marked, the counter was not level and too far from the wall, and the island top was rough with uneven sides. My discontent was palpable. Firmly, I told them, "I want this replaced and back in two days." Unsurprisingly, meeting this demand proved unattainable. The hinges, intended to be soft close, fell short of the mark, and frustration escalated. I asserted, "It is not my fault," as they reluctantly replaced the hinges, clearly displeased. Not wanting to address the issues again, they resisted further adjustments. Calling for reinforcements, I urged them to contact the manufacturers. To my dismay, I learned, "The hinges are faulty, and I have to replace them in all my other jobs before I can come to you." An exasperation, "Oh no!" escaped my lips. I emphasized that I was the one who flagged the issue, not others. Two more months of waiting ensued before the hinges were finally rectified. The countertops, requiring six rounds of sanding to address flaws, were deemed unreplaceable. Faced with the suggestion to sand out any imperfections, I sighed, realizing the battle for low maintenance had been lost. Months later, as I continued to shuttle between the mainland and Sechelt, the unimaginable occurred. Walking into the house, I discovered nail marks on the cabinets and mysterious circles on the Island. Perplexed and concerned, I promptly called Trish to report the unsettling findings. She and her husband came to inspect, but like me, they were at a loss for words. In an attempt to remedy the situation, we replaced the cupboard doors and sanded the countertop. Little did we know, this peculiar scenario would repeat itself four times, leaving us baffled about the cause.

Descending to the lower level, I noticed circles on the wall that seemingly vanished when photographed. This discovery added to my growing unease. The turning point came when I entered the upstairs washroom at night and began hearing voices and conversations. This was disconcerting and felt profoundly wrong.

My friend Tina offered a plausible explanation, suggesting, "It can be spirits. When the tree fell, it could have disturbed the ground." Pondering this theory, I realized that voices were not a daily occurrence. Seeking a solution, I was given Holy Water and advised to sprinkle it around the house while reciting a prayer, urging the spirits to go toward the light. Taking matters into my own hands, I followed these instructions. Thankfully, the markings on the cupboard doors and counters ceased, bringing relief.

With a sloping driveway, concrete became a necessity. The arrival of gravel and rebar marked the commencement of the project. Executed according to plan, the concrete was textured with ridges for winter traction. To my delight, the driveway was completed on my birthday, a pleasant surprise amid the construction chaos.

At the spritely age of 56, I was pleased that after all that I had endured in my life, I was even able to give advice on how to make changes in building my home.

Chapter 19

Home Sweet Home And The Special Cat

As the finishing touches were put on the house, the time to organize the move-in day arrived. Reflecting on the entire experience, from the initial blueprint to the completed home, I marveled at the journey and the ultimate realization of the finished product.

After the completion of the house, I brought the motorhome back to the trailer park in Surrey, where we had stayed before.

Don's friend called and spoke to me, saying, "I have caught the last kitten." Confused, I asked, "What are you talking about?" Apologetically, he explained, "Oh, sorry, I meant to call my landlord." Curious, I inquired about the kitten's fate. He replied, "I am taking it to the SPCA, where the mom and the rest of the litter went." Alarmed, I asked about the kitten's color. "Gray and white," he responded. Without hesitation, I said, "Bring it here, and we will take it."

As it turned out, the kitten was only two weeks old, unable to drink from a dish, and lacking a rough tongue. Despite these challenges, she was undeniably cute. I named her "Smoky."

Don and Smoky relocated to Sechelt in May 2014, where he found solace in sitting on the island in the kitchen, watching seals and eagles. He loved the peace and quiet as there was hardly anyone living on the street full time, so noise was very minimal. He lived there for four years while I commuted, navigating a series of family tragedies detailed further in the book.

At bedtime, Smoky developed a new habit, choosing to sleep at the bottom of my side of the bed. However, she soon started snuggling up to Don, laying against his lower back or by his chest, a behavior she had never exhibited before. I kept an eye on it and then told Don that we needed to go to the mainland to the Doctor to find out what was happening.

A few weeks later, Don received a diagnosis of cancer. Smoky continued to nestle into his chest, a comforting presence. His pain intensified, and despite our desperate situation, Sechelt Hospital turned us away due to the lack of a regular doctor. It was a challenging time, compounded by inadequate medication that failed to alleviate Don's suffering. I had hoped to join Don in Sechelt, anticipating a time of relaxation and retirement together. However, as fate would have it, the good lord had different plans. In March 2018, I made a move, and in April 2018, he was then diagnosed with brain cancer and went for radiation, but unfortunately, Don passed away in May 2018.

I am so glad that he got four years to enjoy the house with Smoky.

I also had an odd knack for predicting where I'd live in the future. I shared my vision with my mom when I was in my late teens, pinpointing a townhouse in Burnaby, BC, and later, a house in Port Coquitlam, BC, and a place in Sechelt. Why those places? Your guess is as good as mine.

Well, low and behold, I eventually lived in each of those homes and now reside in the home in Sechelt, where we pitched a tent when we were youngsters. Since my predictions, all of the homes I had envisioned living in only changed color or type of siding.

I was surprised to find that everything I thought of in my past would happen in my future.

Chapter 20

Reminiscing Barb

Don was busy running a business, so going on holiday, he suggested that Barb and I go alone. Barb, juggling four jobs and steering the ship of her family, deserved a break. Realizing they couldn't afford it, I told her, "It's not fair that you can't go on holiday. We're doing this, and it's on me." I chose to treat her on different outings such as exploring Harrison Hot Springs, spa outings, Sechelt, and then the Western Caribbean. Seeing her joy made the whole effort worthwhile.

Through various friends of ours, there was a group of 10 of us who wanted to travel together to the Western Caribbean. We started our venture traveling from the Vancouver Via Rail station; we headed to Seattle for an overnight stay. During the train ride, we had an unexpected stop due to a rock slide over the tracks. This prompted Barb to suggest a card game to pass the time. Some of us agreed, and it turned out to be a decent way to kill time. Then, we hopped on a plane to New Orleans before setting sail on a cruise ship.

During our time in New Orleans, our lodging was at a 150-year-old bed and breakfast that had seen a flood during the Tornado that had passed there a few days ago and was repaired.

Barb and I shared a one-room with one bed. When it came to exploring New Orleans, Terry, a friend of ours, took it upon himself to organize a tour. When dining out, the rules were a little quirky at some restaurants, limiting tables to two people each, with the explanation that they got better tips that way. We rolled with it, opting for separate but close tables and understanding the dynamics of the service industry.

The food became an exciting journey. I asked, "Do you have something not spicy?" They offered beans and rice along with various curry dishes. The menu was a blend of African, European, Indian, and Chinese cuisine. On days when we were indecisive, we opted for a surprise selection.

Barb recommended, "Try the beans and rice; it's good." I shrugged, "Not my best choice; I'll stick to bread."

The markets fascinated us with raw meat hanging and veggies displayed outside. You could point at what you wanted and decide whether to take it home or have it prepared. Concerned about the raw meat, Barb commented, "It's not healthy." I compromised, "Let's stick to meat and vegetables only."

The clothing stores caught Barb's attention; she was awestruck. I asked, "What's wrong?" She replied, "The clothes are amazing; it's a tough choice for some." I settled for a blouse with front embroidery and drawstring pants— light cotton, one size fits all.

Leaving town, our tour took us to an alligator farm boasting rare white and yellow gators. The guide then proposed a swamp adventure to see more gators. With unanimous agreement, we found ourselves on a large airboat with a massive fan at the back, adding an extra dash of speed to our swamp exploration.

The tour guide threw out a challenge, "Who wants to pet a baby gator?" Despite the temptation, fear got the better of me, and I was the lone holdout. Barb, ever the encourager, chimed in, "Don't be scared; it's time. I'll sit beside you with it." My response? A firm "No way!" followed by her laughter.

Relieved when the gator encounter was over, our next journey took us through the hurricane-ravaged area that had been hit a few years back. Witnessing the aftermath of the tornado's destructive path was sobering—homes torn apart, graveyards in shambles, and signs on doors detailing casualties at each location. The water's reach onto the homes and the stories of resilience left Barb and me feeling a mix of sadness and empathy for the residents.

Every Friday brought a small Mardi Gras night, and it was a captivating experience. Dancers and performers filled the streets, tossing long necklaces to the crowd. As we strolled, Barb pointed out an extraordinary house, describing it as resembling a wedding cake—pure white and intricately decorated. I asked her, "Do you have enough necklaces?" She replied, "No, I am trying to get one of every color."

The next day, we walked and took a bus around town and did more shopping.

After an enjoyable stint in New Orleans, it was time to unwind and embark on the boat for the next leg of our journey.

Our ports of call included Belize, Cozumel, Honduras, and Roatan. Unfortunately, during our Western Caribbean cruise, I had to remain on the boat throughout due to a heat-induced reaction, exacerbating my breathing issues from nerve damage and my use of Lyrica.

While I stayed back, Barb and the rest of the group dove into various activities such as zip lining, snorkeling through caves, bus tours, and more. Barb, in particular, reveled in the experiences, expressing, "I am having so much fun; I do not want this to stop." Her enjoyment ranged from buying intricately hand-carved soap shaped like a lizard to purchasing coffee and simply relishing the moment.

When we docked in Cozumel, the weather was more favorable, and the heat was less oppressive, allowing me to venture off the boat. The entire group explored Cozumel together, creating shared memories. However, our adventure took an unexpected turn when we found ourselves caught in a sudden, intense rainstorm. Seeking refuge in shops, we laughed uncontrollably as we got drenched. The downpour was short-lived, but witnessing Barb's laughter and relaxation was a welcome sight.

During our visit, we received coupons for a diamond shop, prompting me to ask, "Who wants to go to the diamond shop?" Only the women showed interest. Barb excitedly called me over, showcasing a tempting offer – a tennis bracelet adorned with sizable diamonds for just $200. Intrigued, we all gathered around, and Barb, captivated by the deal, decided to purchase both the bracelet and matching earrings.

After our time ashore, it was time to reboard the boat and set our course for home. Exhausted from our adventures, we collectively embraced some quiet moments on the ship, allowing ourselves to rest and recharge.

Expressing her gratitude, Barb remarked, "I thank you all for a wonderful holiday; it is just what we all needed." For me, seeing her happiness was the ultimate reward.

A subsequent girls' weekend took us to the Harrison Hot Springs Spa and Resort, a retreat filled with relaxation in mineral pools, special meals, afternoon high tea, soothing music, and leisurely moments in the lounge. Our time extended to exploring Harrison Hot Springs for shopping and meals, creating cherished memories, and having a lot of fun.

Reflecting on our lives, we acknowledged the missed opportunities of our earlier years but made up for them in our adulthood. Anytime was deemed a good time to come together.

Barb's part-time work as a bookkeeper at the Seafare Mission in the Port of Vancouver, BC, kept her occupied. Additionally, she was part of a team of six people managing a small store at DeltaPort in Point Roberts, BC, catering to sailors and crew. Operating as a nonprofit, the organization relied on donations to sustain its operations.

At the Roberts Bank, BC location, they stocked up on practical items for the sailors – stuffed animals, second-hand jackets, various clothes, gloves, hats, and rain gear. The selection also included food items like chips, cookies, chocolate bars, soups, books, and games. Donations from different people ensured that clothes were available for purchase at a minimal cost, often under five dollars and sometimes even free. They even provided internet access for two dollars a night, allowing sailors to connect with their families and friends back home. Additionally, there were new clothes for purchase.

The sailors developed a fondness for stuffed animals, finding comfort in cuddling with them during the lengthy and sometimes intimidating voyages. In the winter, the store offered winter jackets, hats, mitts, sweaters, and toques lovingly crafted by seniors from local churches. When the sailors questioned the purpose of these winter items, the response was straightforward – "It gets cold, and it will be freezing on the boat for you." These unfamiliar pieces of clothing became essential for their comfort in colder weather.

Barb took an extra step by reaching out to the sailors, asking, "Is there anything besides what's on this list that you would like for the next time you come here?" The sailors responded with specific requests, and Barb made sure to fulfill them. Their gratitude was evident as they expressed amazement and appreciation for her efforts.

Barb's contributions went beyond clothing. She brought in essential items such as perfume, laundry soap, deodorant, and personal supplies. Recognizing the sailors' needs, she also stocked up on groceries like pancake mix, syrup, cereals, and crackers, along with practical items like phone cards to make calling home more affordable, Zippo lighters, and watches. These thoughtful additions aimed to make the sailors' lives a bit more comfortable during their time at sea.

The sailors often remarked, "Barb, this is the best-stocked place out of all our stops around the world." In response, Barb would say, "We want you to feel at home."

Barb took it upon herself to make this place a haven for the sailors. She scoured Dollarama, Dollar Tree, Shoppers Drug Mart, and grocery stores, leaving no limit on what she could bring in. With every purchase, she accumulated points, which she then used for additional buys and Christmas supplies.

Even the managers at Dollarama and Dollar Tree recognized Barb's dedication. They offered to streamline the process, saying, "Barb, you place your order with us, and we will order the same stuff." Barb's response was pragmatic, "Why? Because you know what to order."

Working only three days a week, Barb made her shopping rounds in the mornings, ensuring that she would bring in the goods by 2 pm when the store opened. The demand was evident as a line would often form before the opening. Recognizing the workload, Barb would occasionally seek my help, asking, "Eileen, can you help this week to put the goods away as I have a huge carload of goods." I gladly agreed, always responding with a "Yes!"

The store witnessed a steady stream of visitors, ranging from 20 to 40 people at any given time. It wasn't just the sailors; the captain, engineers, and others would also frequent the place. Barb's commitment made it not just a store but a comforting retreat for those spending time away from home.

Barb's resourcefulness extended beyond provisions; she scoured Craigslist for various games to keep the sailors entertained. One day, she called me, saying, "I have a shuffleboard. Can you help me with it?" I, like the sailors, was always amazed at what she managed to find.

The store was more than just a place to shop; it was a haven for the sailors. Sofas provided a spot to relax and watch TV, while large tables accommodated laptops and games. A separate area equipped with phones offered a quiet space for conversations with friends and family. Refreshments were on the house – complimentary tea or coffee and cookies. Juice, pop, and ice cream were also available for purchase.

When Christmas approached, we organized a festive party complete with a tree, food, and gifts. Generous donations from different companies included items like small duffle bags, toothpaste, toothbrushes, shaving cream, cookies, hair shampoo, knitted hats, mitts, socks, and more.

Barb's warmth and dedication earned her the sailors' affection. Occasionally, the Captain would invite her for dinner, surprising her with unfamiliar dishes – a challenge she embraced with an open mind.

The sailors had grown fond of a budgie that was a fixture at the store. However, one day, the bird was no longer there. When asked, Barb revealed, "It died, but we are getting a cat." This announcement startled the sailors, but Barb, resourceful as ever, applied to the SPCA for an older, calm tabby cat. The cat became a beloved companion, finding comfort on counters and sailors' laps.

It became a link to home, with sailors calling their families and proudly showing them their feline friends.

Roberts Bank held a special place in the sailors' hearts to the extent that they would inquire about the destination before accepting a job. If it wasn't headed to Roberts Bank, they weren't interested.

Sailors from around the world, on coal or container ships, frequented the store. Container ships mainly hailed from Europe, while coal ships arrived from China, Vietnam, the Philippines, and beyond.

Life and pay on the container ship offered a better experience compared to the coal ship. The coal ship was a gritty environment with coal dust pervasive, and the pay wasn't great, but it was a job. Sleeping at the bottom of the boat came with its challenges, described by the sailors as "very noisy and scary" during storms with high waves crashing against the vessel.

In an effort to provide comfort, we offered rosaries for the sailors to take and keep with them when they went to bed. Additionally, we had a collection of Christian books and Bibles that they would often take along.

The sailors, mainly in the age range of 16 to 30ish, endured long stretches at sea, often exceeding nine months. It was a poignant reality as they missed significant life events, including the births of their children, family gatherings, deaths, and special occasions.

Barb assumed a maternal role for the sailors, and they looked up to her as someone they could confide in. Her infectious happiness had a reassuring effect, making them feel better even in challenging times.

When Barb passed away on February 18, 2016, the sailors, accustomed to seeing her at the store, came in and noticed her absence. They inquired about her, only to be met with the devastating news that she had been killed in a car accident.

Shocked and uncertain, they grappled with the sudden absence of the familiar and uplifting presence. The void left by Barb's passing was deeply felt by the sailors who had come to see her as a beacon of support and warmth.

She was taken too soon. She left behind two sons, 19 and 20 years of age. I was now their "go-to person." I helped to direct them in their life choices and their parents' estate.

Chapter 21

Family Tragedies

Between January 2015 and May 2018, my life was hit with a series of devastating losses. It started with the passing of my father, who was 87 years old. Then, I lost my sister, who was only 49 at the time, along with my beloved 14-year-old cocker spaniel. Shortly after, my longtime tenant, Bobby, passed away at 65. The string of losses continued with the passing of my mother at 82 and then my husband, who was 64. We had been married for 29 years.

It was an unimaginable and overwhelming period of loss and grief. Coping with so much loss in such a short time was incredibly difficult. I had to rely on my faith in God and my own inner strength to get through each day.

Dealing with all the closures and losses was incredibly tough, and I had to handle most of it on my own. There wasn't much help or support from others during that challenging time.

Chapter 22

An Unexpected Turn

Later on, Smoky, the feline companion, seemed to sense changes in my health. Interestingly, during this time, Smoky, our feral cat, began displaying unusual behavior. She started snuggling up to me at night, a habit previously reserved for my late husband, Don, and now she even nudged me, creating a newfound closeness. To this day, Smoky continues to sleep with me, and when I sleep on my back, she is lying on my chest just to make sure I am breathing. If I am upset, she will snuggle by my side while offering comfort.

Her shifts in behavior by laying on my stomach prompted me to seek medical advice. Just when I thought things couldn't get any worse, I received the devastating news: I was diagnosed with cancer, and after a biopsy, it led to the discovery of Uterus cancer, leading to a necessary hysterectomy.

The doctors said that the stress I had been through with all the closures and losses likely played a big role in causing the cancer. It felt like a heavy blow, adding to the already overwhelming burden I was carrying. But I knew I had to stay strong and face this new challenge head-on.

The cancer diagnosis in October 2018, initially at stage one, progressed to stage two by the time of the surgery in April 2019, a realization I had not been aware of prior to the medical intervention.

In 2019, I underwent two rounds of chemotherapy, opting not to pursue radiation therapy. Despite recommendations from the Vancouver Cancer Clinic for a more intensive treatment plan involving radiation, I chose not to proceed with the additional rounds, prioritizing a less invasive approach to my recovery. Currently, I am cancer-free, grateful for catching the condition early and navigating the journey on my terms.

Facing a challenging health situation, I sought out a second opinion through prayer and the support of friends. Margaret, a friend, connected me with a cancer specialist, Dr. Klemo, who is known for his innovative approach and experience in working with cancer patients. At 84 years old, he was still practicing in North Vancouver. However, by the time I consulted him, I had already undergone unnecessary chemotherapy following my hysterectomy. Dr. Klemo expressed regret, stating that I did not require any treatment after the surgery and that my cancer was from all the stress I endured through the passing of my family members and dealing with finalizing their estate.

The timing, albeit unfortunate, turned out to be a strange stroke of luck, as Dr. Klemo retired after my last visit. Since then, I've remained cancer-free from 2019 onward.

The peculiar part of my journey involved Smoky, a feral and independent cat not known for being people-friendly. However, she turned out to be an unexpected blessing, sensing when something was amiss and becoming a constant presence, even sleeping at the foot of my bed.

Chapter 23

Miracles at Work

In this chapter, I recount the transformative experiences of witnessing individuals undergoing the Bilateral Nasal Specific Technique, a therapy that holds the promise of profound change.

1) One such tale revolves around a dear family friend's son, Bruce. From a young age, Bruce faced significant challenges due to his mental condition, requiring constant support and guidance from his parents just to navigate the simplest tasks. His world was one of dependence, where even the act of walking necessitated the presence of his father leading him with treats, coaxing him forward step by step.

It was against this backdrop of struggle that my parents shared with Bruce's family the possibility of hope offered by Dr. Stober in Portland, Oregon. With newfound optimism, Bruce's parents eagerly reached out to Dr. Stober's office, setting in motion a journey that would change their lives forever.

The anticipation mounted as they made the journey to Portland for their appointment. With each passing mile, their hopes soared, fueled by the prospect of a breakthrough. And when they finally crossed the threshold into Dr. Stober's office, they were met with a ray of hope in the form of a single assurance: "Yes, I can help him."

With those words, a new chapter began for Bruce and his family. The treatments commenced two weeks later, becoming a regular fixture in their lives for the next six months. The specifics of the therapy— the number of finger cots used, the frequency of sessions— remain shrouded in uncertainty, but what emerged was undeniable: a transformation unfolding before their very eyes.

Slowly but surely, Bruce began to defy the limitations that once bound him. No longer reliant on constant guidance, he found newfound independence, grasping onto his parents' hands as he ventured forth into uncharted territory— walking on his own accord.

The stories of miraculous transformations through the Bi-Lateral Nasal Specific Technique continue to inspire and astound.

One such tale revolves around a young boy named Bruce, whose life took a dramatic turn following the treatment. His newfound freedom allowed him to embark on adventures he could only dream of before. One particularly harrowing incident stands out—when Bruce's friend fell through the ice while ice fishing, he didn't hesitate to plunge in after him, saving both their lives. It's a testament to the profound impact the treatment had, granting him the ability to act decisively in a moment of crisis.

2) Similarly, the journey of twin girls born with caved-in heads speaks to the transformative power of the technique. Born with their skulls pressed against each other in the womb, their future seemed bleak until their mother sought out a Naturopath skilled in the cranial technique. Through a series of treatments, the girls' heads gradually began to reshape, restoring hope and happiness to their families.

3) But the journey doesn't end there. Dr. Kelly Farnsworth, recognizing the potential for further miracles, extended a helping hand to a family with a son diagnosed with Down syndrome. Through mentorship and guidance, coupled with the cranial treatments, they witnessed remarkable improvements in the boy's facial features in just a matter of weeks. However, their joy was tempered by the skepticism of the husband's brother, a chiropractor from Alberta, who denounced the treatments, casting doubt on their efficacy.

The decision weighed heavy on Mom's shoulders as she grappled with conflicting emotions and pressures from all sides. Despite the remarkable progress her son was making with the Bi-Lateral Nasal Specific Cranial Technique, the disapproval of both the Down syndrome association and her brother-in-law cast a shadow of doubt on the treatment's validity.

As the treatments continued, the improvements became more apparent, offering glimpses of hope for a brighter future. However, when faced with the scrutiny of external authorities and familial opinions, Mom made the difficult choice to halt the treatments. The fear of alienation and judgment outweighed the potential benefits her son could have gained from continued therapy.

I pleaded with her to reconsider, emphasizing the transformative impact the treatment had already demonstrated. I urged her to prioritize her son's well-being and the possibility of a more fulfilling life over the opinions of others. Ultimately, Mom chose to prioritize familial harmony over potential medical advancements, a decision born out of love and a desire to protect her family's relationships.

4) Despite the setback, the ripple effect of the cranial technique's success continued to touch lives. I shared my own story with a co-worker, Cindy, who had long suffered from jaw issues. Encouraged by my experience, she sought out Dr. Kelly for treatment. To her amazement, after just a few sessions, her jaw realigned itself, putting an end to her years of discomfort.

5) I met Jan Rogers Wimberley, author, in May 2024 in Portland, Oregon, for a treatment.

Her soon to be published book:

"The Unprejudiced Mind."

It will not only warm your heart but also offer a self-help and resource book. With "No Help" ringing in their ears from their medical doctors, these parents discover the importance and wide application of chiropractic Bilateral Nasal Specific skull bone manipulation - the procedure which changes the expected mental retardation of Hurler Syndrome to "extremely bright." More surprise awaits when they discover a nutritional formula is reversing the symptoms of Down Syndrome! Will this also help their son, Jimmy?

The purpose of her book is to encourage others going through devastating circumstances and to let the world know these treatments and nutrition can help major or minor and multiple chronic health problems.

Suffering has been relieved from sinus issues, headaches, and simple or severe head injuries from accidents, sports, birth, or military service. If I worked for a little boy whose genetics were not all there, what would it do for those who are not missing a gene in each cell of their bodies

6) Now, reflecting on my own journey, I am reminded of the countless miracles that have shaped my life from the same treatment. From overcoming immense struggles in every aspect. I have experienced the full spectrum of life's challenges and blessings. With the unwavering support of loved ones, determination, and faith, I have been near death to having ascended the steepest of hills to reach the pinnacle of contentment and fulfillment - for which I am so grateful.

Chapter 24

My new life as a single

Volunteering at the Therapeutic Riding Association in Sechelt, B.C., was a fulfilling chapter of my life. Run by Sandra, who cared for three Arabian horses—Mady, Fiona, and Tara—the center focused on helping riders regain strength, addressing conditions like cerebral palsy, ADHD, autism, etc.

I witnessed the joy and improvement they experienced through horseback riding, and Sandra guided them through various movements and exercises, enhancing their speech by applying pressure to prompt the horse to move or say, "Walk On."

She would have people leading horses and assisting disabled riders with exercises that became a rewarding routine, from reaching for a horse's tail to stretching, throwing balls into buckets, reaching up on the mane, and engaging in arm rotations. These activities not only helped riders physically but also played a role in enhancing their confidence, balance, muscle tone, and speech. Witnessing the positive impact on riders within just a few sessions was remarkable. Volunteering in this environment not only allows me to enjoy working with horses but also brings immense satisfaction in witnessing the smiles and accomplishments of riders facing various medical challenges. It's a fulfilling experience that goes beyond the physical aspects, fostering a sense of independence and connection between the riders and their equine companions. Witnessing the pride of the riders is genuinely heartwarming, emphasizing the remarkable impact a horse can have on their lives.

Unfortunately, my involvement in this meaningful work had to be cut short due to the challenges posed by my own health. Dealing with pain from Complex Regional Pain Syndrome (CRPS) became increasingly difficult, exacerbated by exposure to varying weather conditions during the sessions. Additionally, the medication (Lyrica) prescribed for CRPS led to Bronchiectasis, making it hard to endure the dust and allergens from the stable environment. Amidst these struggles, subsequent treatments added further complexity, making it necessary for me to step back from my dream job.

Remaining in Sechelt, I joined various groups, including Newcomers, Walking, and a Grief Counseling group. These engagements led me to form meaningful friendships with some outstanding individuals who, like me, are navigating life as singles. From coffee sessions and games to walks and shopping trips, having these friends in my life has been a valuable support system, providing companionship and shared experiences.

In a surprising turn of events, a decision to join a walking group on a day that led to a pivotal encounter. Post-walk coffee introductions introduced me to Dale, and from that moment, it felt like we were kindred spirits. As members of the walking group, we discovered shared interests and a connection that went beyond the ordinary.

Dale, a seasoned journalist with a repertoire of articles and short stories, was in the process of writing a book. Sharing my own venture into autobiography writing, he expressed genuine excitement upon learning the details of my life story. Dale has brought inspiration, happiness, understanding, fulfillment, and peace, embodying a profound connection.

Dale and I met in February 2019, a period marked by the challenges of my ongoing cancer diagnosis.

Now that I am cancer-free, we can start our new adventure. Dale's book, "Meant to Be," will be published in May 2024. It is about Love, Life, and Living on the Beautiful Sunshine Coast.

Chapter 25

New-found treatment

To add to the pain, in 2019, my Naturopath, Dr. Kelly Farnsworth, was in a tragic motorcycle accident that left him unable to work again.

During this time, I desperately needed a cranial treatment to help me cope with the emotional and physical toll of everything I was going through. Unfortunately, I couldn't find anyone nearby who could provide the treatment I needed.

Fast forward five years from my last treatment, I stumbled upon a new type of therapy called Biodynamic Craniosacral Therapy. It was totally unfamiliar to me, but I figured I'd give it a shot and see how it goes.

This therapy is quite unique. It's not about manipulation or forceful movements. Instead, it's all about tapping into the natural energies within our bodies that promote health and well-being. It actually traces its origins back to the early days of Osteopathy cranial work.

The idea behind it is to work with these natural energies to help the body heal itself. It's like giving a gentle nudge to our nervous system, supporting it in finding balance and harmony.

What's interesting is that it's not just about physical health; it also draws from psychology and neuroscience. It considers how our early life experiences and traumas might affect our well-being later on.

So, I decided to give it a try, curious to see how this holistic approach could help me. And who knows, maybe it'll provide some relief and support for my body and mind.

I met Martha after I got a concussion from a bad fall. Someone suggested I see her for help. Martha's approach to therapy is gentle and doesn't involve any harsh techniques. She uses a light touch to connect with the body's natural healing abilities.

My session with Martha was amazing. It lasted about 90 minutes, during which she placed her warm hands on different parts of my body. She waited patiently to see if my body responded with any movement or verbal cues. Then, she would move on to another area.

After the treatment, I felt incredible. I went home and slept for 24 hours straight! But it wasn't just any sleep; it felt like my body was really soaking in the effects of the therapy.

Over time, I noticed some remarkable changes. The pressure in my forehead decreased, my toes straightened out (they'd been curled up from my concussion), my cheekbones became more prominent, and my eyes seemed to align better. Plus, I felt like a weight had been lifted off my shoulders, and I had more energy.

I was blown away by how much this treatment helped me. It's incredible to think that such a gentle touch could bring about such significant improvements.

This treatment is used for a lot of health problems like migraines, disturbed sleep, back and neck pain, concussions, vertigo, etcetera.

About a month after my last therapy session with Martha, I decided to go back to see her. During the session, she noticed something interesting - my left eye seemed more open, and my left cheekbone had a rosy tint, indicating some movement. It was fascinating to see these subtle changes.

After the session, though, I was completely wiped out. I felt so exhausted that I ended up sleeping for a solid 12 hours straight. It seemed like my body needed time to process everything that had happened.

Curious to explore more options for my recovery, I started searching online. I came across a chiropractor who still practiced the Bi-Lateral Nasal Specific Technique.

I had the opportunity to travel to the USA with my girlfriend, Liz, so I could receive treatment. I was hopeful that this new treatment would bring further relief and progress in my healing journey.

I had three treatments, and the same technique was used where he attached one finger cot to the blood pressure ball and wrapped it with dental floss to secure it so it would not come off. He then inserted it into each of the six passages in my nose one at a time. Unfortunately, most of the passages were blocked, so he added two more and eventually three finger cots in order to open up all the passages. It was a relief when all the passages finally opened again, especially considering how my concussion had messed up my system. After the treatments, I went back to my hotel room feeling pretty sore. The sides of my head and back were all achy, making it hard to sleep. I asked about the pain on the day, and he explained that my body had a lot of blockages and the treatment was putting everything back in its place. He reassured me that it would take time for things to settle.

Saturday's treatment went well, and that night, I finally went to sleep; I crashed hard. Surprisingly, I didn't feel any pain, which was a huge relief. It seemed like the therapy was starting to work its magic slowly but surely.

The day after my last treatment with Liz, I embarked on a long drive back home to Sechelt, B.C. Once I got home, I crashed into bed and slept for a whopping 36 hours straight. Even after all that rest, I still felt incredibly tired for a couple of days afterward.

I'm really thankful that Liz came along for the ride. Having her there for company and support was a huge comfort, especially since I wasn't sure how I'd feel after the treatment.

Now that I'm back home, I'll need to go back in about three months. It's important to keep tabs on my progress and make sure everything's on track.

I feel incredibly grateful to have found someone to help me and continue these treatments; I won't have to wait another six years before seeking help again. It's a relief to know that I can continue with the treatments and keep making progress on my healing journey.

Acknowledgments

Reflecting on the journey, I realize that my life has been touched by numerous miracles—from experiencing a whole life to encountering two soulmates and residing in a place characterized by tranquility and calm. Each step forward represents a triumph over adversity, and with every passing day, a newfound appreciation for life emerges. Surviving and overcoming the worst challenges, I attribute my resilience to prayer and the blessings I've received. Despite the hardships, struggles, and losses, I am alive and content today. Maintaining a positive outlook through the ups and downs has been my guiding force. Now, with my soulmate, friends, and faith in God, I am ready to savor life. I consider myself a living miracle, a unique survivor with a story that defies the odds.

Reflecting on the incredible support, I can confidently assert that I am the luckiest person in the world to have such a solid group of individuals who stood by me throughout my journey.

Though saddened by the loss of Dr. Earl, Dr. Fleming, and Dr. Stober, as well as my beloved grandparents and parents, their legacies continue to inspire and uplift me every day. They are forever cherished in my thoughts and prayers.

Cheeks have shifted needing cranial treatment to straighten eye

As you have now read this account, I leave you with a question: *Do you believe* ***"Miracles Do Happen?***

If you have any questions, please feel free to reach out to me at: miraclesdohappenyes@gmail.com